London No.1
is proudly sponsored by
the following partners

DRWakefield

EST.1970

COFFEE MACHINES

DELICIOUSLY CORNISH DAIRY

FOR BREW FRE &BEA GEEK

Editor
Selena Young

Editorial team
Abi Manning
Melissa Morris
Jane Rakison
Rosanna Rothery
Phil Wain
Lara Watson

Editorial director
Jo Rees

Design
Tom Hampton
Dale Stiling

Commercial
Owen Penrice
Mark Tibbles

Publishing
Charlotte Cummins
Tamsin Powell

Managing director
Nick Cooper

Big thanks to the *Indy Coffee Guide* committee
(meet them on page 14) for their expertise and
enthusiasm, and to our partners: DRWakefield,
Sanremo and Trewithen.

Coffee shops, cafes and roasteries are invited
to be included in the guide based on meeting
criteria set by the committee, which includes the
use of speciality beans, providing a high-quality
coffee experience for visitors and being
independently run.

For information on *Indy Coffee Guides* visit:

indycoffee.guide

 indycoffeeguide

© Salt Media Ltd
Published by Salt Media Ltd 2024

saltmedia.co.uk | 01271 859299
ideas@saltmedia.co.uk

Contents

WELCOME

We're thrilled to bring you the first edition of *Indy Coffee Guide London*.

This publication has been a long time coming. During the past decade, we've created over 25 editions of the *Indy Coffee Guide*, covering practically every other area of the UK and Ireland.

London was the missing puzzle piece in our portfolio so it's been our pleasure to fix that by delving into the capital's vibrant coffee scene. As with each of our guides, our aim is to reveal to our readers the very best indie cafes, coffee shops and roasteries dealing in speciality* coffee.

To decide which venues were worth shouting about, our coffee-mad team undertook a tour of the best coffee destinations (tough work, we admit). We also deliberated with our committee of industry pros (meet them on page 14). So rest assured that this cherry-picked selection won't let you down.

Every venue included in the guide meets the criteria of serving (or roasting) speciality-grade coffee, being independently owned, offering

multiple brew methods or guest roasts and generally being a pleasing place to sink a proper brew.

In addition to doling out world-class coffee, many cafes in the guide serve incredible food. Other dynamic spots have hybrid set-ups and incorporate bakeries, co-working spaces, restaurants, retail and studios. One even has a pinball arcade ...

As you hunt out these unique finds, be sure to tag us; we love to see our guides doing their work in the wild.

Of course, this isn't an exhaustive list of everywhere you'll find speciality in the city, but it's a damn good collection which'll take your coffee drinking next-level. Slide into our DMs if there's a cafe or roastery you think should be included in the next edition.

Selena Young

Editor

@ indycoffeeguide

A few of the *Indy Coffee Guide* team.
L-R: Tamsin, Selena, Charlotte, Chris, Dale, Nick and Mark

© Guy Harrop

SHOP

View our entire range of
guides at **indycoffee.guide**

L-R: Wales; England: South; Ireland; Scotland;
England: North, Midlands & East.

What is speciality coffee?

Speciality coffee beans are those that have been graded above 80 on
a 100-point scale (set by the Speciality Coffee Association) for quality.

 80 ⟷ 100

These beans often come from small farms across the world's coffee-growing belt,
and are cultivated in select altitudes and climates by farmers who nurture the crops
with great attention to detail. Q graders assess these coffees, determining if they
make the grade to be classed as speciality.

Once speciality beans land at roasteries in the UK, they're roasted lightly to preserve
their specific characteristics which represent the terroir in which they were grown.

Speciality green coffee beans are significantly more expensive to source than
regular commodity coffee, so are treated with great care by baristas: grinding,
brewing and serving the beans in a way that respects the journey from origin to cup.

Meet the
COMMITTEE

The *Indy Coffee Guide* team work with a group of industry experts to identify the best cafes and roasteries to feature in the guide

Maxwell Colonna-Dashwood

Maxwell's fascination with speciality coffee was ignited in Melbourne, Australia, in 2007. On return to the UK, he set up a coffee events company and then, in 2009, opened Colonna & Small's on Bath's Chapel Row.

A three-time UK Barista Champion, Maxwell is a thought-leader in the industry. He is a co-author on several academic papers on coffee and has published a series of books on the subject, including his latest: *The Business of Speciality Coffee*.

Bruna Costa

As a result of growing up in a coffee-industry family in Brazil, Bruna has the business in her blood and has dabbled in many elements of the coffee world – from roasting and researching to exporting and importing. In 2018, she moved to London to manage an import company but has now started Bossa Coffee Company, a relationship-focused coffee importer.

Tom Sixsmith

Since scoring his first speciality job in Vancouver in 2011, Tom has undertaken a huge range of roles in the industry and in a number of cities around the world. Most notably he ran Origin Coffee's Shoreditch shop, Nomad in Barcelona and Society Cafe in Oxford. In 2021, he opened Batch Baby in East London with partner Saskia Blum.

Jack Ravenscroft

Jack's coffee journey began in 2014 when he started working behind the bar of a speciality cafe in South London. His career since has spanned sustainability, cold brew and green coffee. In 2022, he joined the team at DRWakefield as a coffee trader.

Saskia Blum

Aussie Saskia began working in coffee at a young age, pulling shots as a part-time barista between her school studies. Then, in 2019, after doing stints at some of Europe's best coffee shops, she settled in London where she worked at Store Street Espresso before going on to manage Pavilion Cafe in Victoria Park. In 2021, she opened Batch Baby in East London with partner Tom Sixsmith.

Aashifa Hussein

A graduate of the Well Grounded trainee programme, Aashifa has been working in speciality coffee since 2016. She's now a senior trainer at the community interest company, which offers training for people facing barriers to employment. Alongside her role, she's also an advisor for The Barista League and has written for *Caffeine Magazine*.

What's special about
LONDON'S
speciality?

Coffee writer Phil Wain takes the temperature of the capital's speciality scene and finds some exciting developments at London's indie coffee shops and cafes

© Jamie Lau

London has been at the forefront of the UK independent speciality coffee scene since the mid-2000s and the scene continues to evolve and excite.

Indie coffee shops have a lot to compete with these days as there are so many places serving speciality brews: pubs, restaurants and even nail bars and hairdressers are serving up flat whites. The high-street coffee chains have raised their game, too.

Considering this, let's celebrate the continued successes of independent cafes – those owned by families and individuals as opposed to multinational corporations. And while many have gone under, others have competed by elevating their offering.

A David and Goliath story

There are a number of ways small businesses can outcompete Costa, Starbucks and Caffè Nero. At a great indie cafe you'll enjoy creative interior design and feast on homemade food made with care. Often, brews are made by the person who created and nurtured the cafe, which provides a unique hospitality experience.

It's not for everyone of course; some people crave the familiarity of the large-chain experience, but the readers of this guide will be those who seek out the unusual, the creative and the artisan.

How to find the good stuff

In a London suffused with speciality coffee, there is a premium on recommendation, such as that provided by this guide. With so many coffee shops on the capital's streets, it's not easy to simply stumble on the most special or authentic spots.

I've always felt that during the working day – whether in the office, at home or elsewhere – the coffee break is a transcendent experience. The ritual of brewing and drinking coffee has the unique ability to transform the day – if only for a few minutes. Visiting a coffee shop can take you out of the here and now, reduce stress and provide a moment of pleasure.

While many London venues meet expectations, some deliver something more unique, in which a quality cup or a distinctive environment takes the experience next-level.

All change

More recently, there have been trends in how indie coffee shops craft these unique experiences. Some have created an exceptional atmosphere through design – such as in Asian-influenced sites like Kuro in Notting Hill and Nagare in Spitalfields. Others, like Saint Nine in Southwark, transform their location through the use of murals and artwork, or, like Profile in Highbury, make clever use of space in a small shop.

Lockdown shifted the focus to takeaway service and some have further expanded in this direction, prioritising fast service. Others embraced the return to normal life by concentrating on the slow pleasures of the sit-in experience.

Some cafes, like SHED Clapham, welcome workers in search of wifi while others such as Local Hero in Teddington have promoted socialisation with like-minded enthusiasts such as runners. Then there are the coffee shops like Colonna & Small's which have created a space where customers can take a deep dive into the world of high-octane speciality caffeine. Diversity of offer is what makes the speciality scene so special.

Coffee, community and collabs

The importance of the local community coffee shop has also increased now that more people work from home. Coffee shops in residential areas meet locals' needs and pride themselves on developing friendly rapport with their regulars – Kaffeine in Fitzrovia and Lodestar in Clapton are typical examples.

Independent roasteries have also flourished in recent years and London has its fair share of artisan roasters bronzing beans from far-flung corners of the globe.

Some cafes, such as Intermission in Hampstead, Party at Pavilion in Chelsea and Tamp Coffee in Chiswick, showcase own-roasted beans. Others, such as Paradox in Westgate Street, Batch Baby in De Beauvoir and Store Street Espresso in Bloomsbury, feature top-drawer roasteries on rotation and attract knowledgeable speciality fans and pro baristas who visit to select from a smorgasbord of beans – and purchase bags of coffee from the retail section.

At its best, London's independent speciality coffee scene has always been a collaborative one. That's naturally changed a little as the scene has grown from a handful of businesses to many hundreds over the past 15 years, but it's noticeable that there's a small but marked effort being made by businesses to draw the coffee community together. Examples include Kaffeine's annual latte art competition, Batch Baby and Paradox's collaboration and a recent event featuring Okinawan coffee roasters, along with events at Saint Espresso and Moonstruck.

Party at Pavilion

Small but deadly

Hospitality is having a hard time due to rising energy and food costs, and recruitment issues, and we've seen some larger speciality chains go under. However, being a smaller independent business does provide flexibility and the freedom to pivot quickly, which can provide some protection.

The independents may not have the financial muscle and scale to survive all the financial knocks, but they have some advantages and have competed with the corporate chains by upping their game and providing many types of unique experience. And it's London's coffee drinkers who benefit.

How to use
the GUIDE.

Coffee shops

Discover full page and shot-size write-ups of coffee shops and cafes where you can drink top-notch coffee.

We've split the guide into geographical areas of North, East, South, Central and West (based on the London Plan maps) to help you find speciality spots near you.

Roasteries

Meet leading speciality coffee roasters and discover where to source beans. Find them in the roasteries section.

Maps

Every cafe and roastery is numbered and marked on the map at the start of each section of the guide.

Follow us on Instagram
🔘 indycoffeeguide

KEY

Symbols at the bottom of each cafe and roastery page provide further information on what you'll find at the venue.

Wifi

Dogs welcome

Bike friendly

Reusables accepted

Buy beans in store

Buy beans online

Outdoor seating

Cafe at the roastery

Roastery open to the public

Roastery visit by invite

Coffee courses

One of multiple sites

Espresso Redefined:

Explore our extensive collection of premium espresso machines

Visit the South Kensington showroom & HUB to test drive our
espresso machines tailored for home and professional use.

6/7 Thurloe Place, South Kensington, London

YOUR ADVEN-TURES

START HERE

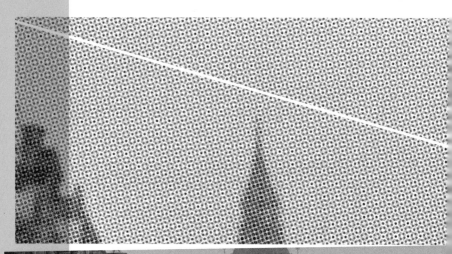

25

Central London cafes

1 Daku Coffee
2 Layla Bakery
3 Klear Labs
4 Hermanos Colombian Coffee Roasters – cafe
5 TAB X TAB
6 Kuro Coffee
7 Notting Hill Coffee Project
8 LIFT
9 Black Rabbit Cafe
10 HJEM Kensington
11 Guillam Coffee House
12 Boxcar Baker & Deli
13 Workshop Coffee
14 Party at Pavilion
15 Kiss the Hippo – Fitzrovia
16 Qima Cafe
17 Saint Espresso – Camden
18 Kaffeine London
19 Kitchen Coffee
20 Caravan – cafe
21 Store St Espresso
22 Omotesando Koffee
23 Lavelle Bike + Bean
24 Söderberg – Soho
25 Café Leon Dore
26 flat white
27 Formative Coffee
28 Iris & June – Victoria
29 Nostos Coffee
30 Gramos Coffee Bar
31 26 Grains
32 Monmouth Coffee Company – Covent Garden
33 Arôme Bakery
34 Redemption Roasters
35 Drury 188-189
36 News & Coffee
37 Meletius Speciality Coffee Roasters
38 Prufrock
39 Devotion Coffee
40 Colonna & Small's
41 Iris & June – Holborn Circus
42 Pickwick Coffee Club
43 Rosslyn – Queen Victoria Street
44 Ozone Coffee – Shoreditch
45 Party at Moorgate
46 Curators Coffee
47 Three Wheels Coffee
48 Rosslyn – London Wall
49 Saint Nine Coffee
50 Lantana
51 Monmouth Coffee Company – The Borough
52 Frequency
53 Big Bro Espresso

Locations are approximate

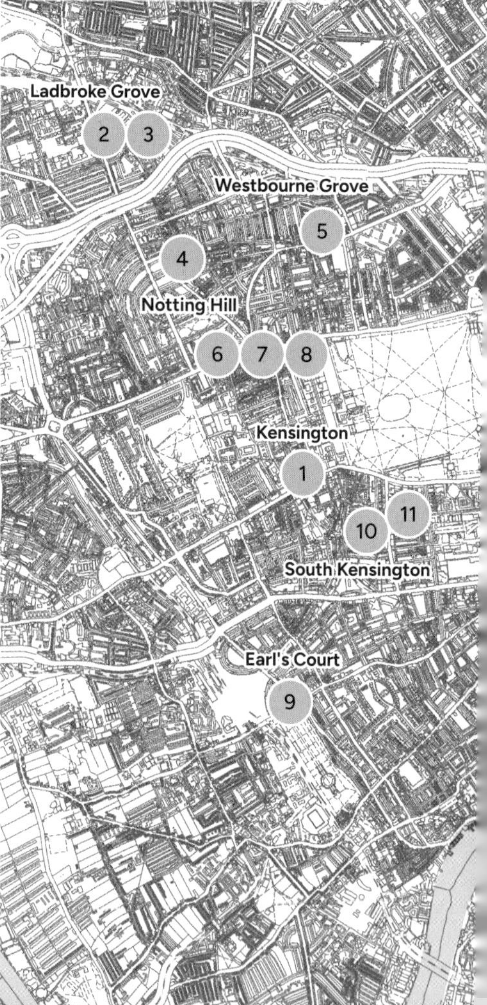

Ladbroke Grove
2
3
Westbourne Grove
5
4
Notting Hill
6
7
8
Kensington
1
11
10
South Kensington
Earl's Court
9

Camden
17
20
King's Cross
30
Clerkenwell
39
Shoreditch
44
16
Bloomsbury
40
Fitzrovia
Farringdon
19
38
Barbican
45
12
21
Marylebone
37
41
48
53
13
36
35
18
22
City of
London
46
15
Holborn
43
Soho
23
Covent Garden
42
Blackfriars
31
24
32
25
33
49
50
47
26
34
51
Southwark
St James's
52
29
27
Westminster
28
14
Chelsea

Find more cafes in this area on the East London map on page 68

27

(1) Daku Coffee

100 Kensington High Street, W8 4SG

dakucoffee.com

f dakucoffee ⓞ daku_coffee

Wickedly fresh coffee is the speciality at this cafe-roastery on Kensington High Street. Just seven days after the latest haul of carefully sourced beans have been bronzed (and allowing for post-roast resting), they're ground and extracted into espresso drinks that demand attention.

The baristas serve the coffee within this tight timeframe to ensure they capture the peak of the beans' freshness and deliver notes that pack a punch.

This meticulous roasting-brewing schedule showcases the nuances of different coffee processing methods. Take note of how the natural-process coffees offer fruity richness and full-bodied flavour, while washed-process beans deliver a clean and vibrant cup with standout notes.

🌀 Artists, it's free to showcase your work in Daku

With Daku's minimalist styling, suave Sanremo Opera and eye-catching artwork on the walls, this is a space where visitors can revel in quality coffee and creativity. Events such as art exhibitions, book clubs and craft workshops take the vibe further and inspire collaboration in the community.

Established
2024

Key roaster
Daku Coffee

Brewing method
Espresso

Machine
Sanremo Opera

Grinder
Sanremo X-ONE

Opening hours
Mon-Fri
7.30am-6pm
Sat
8am-5.30pm
Sun
8.30am-5pm

Layla Bakery

(2) **Layla Bakery**

Good coffee and carbs are perfect bedfellows and two of life's simple pleasures, a fact not lost on the Layla crew who craft beautiful examples of both at this Ladbroke Grove cafe-bakery. Fill your face then stock up on bread and pastries to-go.

332 Portobello Road, Ladbroke Grove, W10 5SA

laylabakery.com | @ layla_w10

(3) **Klear Labs**

Wholesome health-focused food and organic seasonal juices meet quality caffeination at this contemporary 'house of food'. Sustainability, seasonality and flavour are packed into every morsel and sip.

93 Golborne Road, W10 5NL

klear-labs.com | @ klear.labs

(4) **Hermanos Colombian Coffee Roasters** 🎧

Exclusively serving own-roasted Colombian beans, Hermanos' collection of coffee shops includes this Portobello Road site. Grab a coffee to-go as you explore the market, vintage stores and pop-ups.

127 Portobello Road, W11 2DY

hermanoscoffeeroasters.com

@ hermanoscolombiancoffee

(5) **TAB X TAB**

A fifteen-minute walk from Paddington station, or short stroll from Kensington Palace or Hyde Park brings gourmets to alight at this ideally situated brunch spot for superb caffeination and freshly cooked fodder.

14-16 Westbourne Grove, W2 5RH

tabxtab.com | @ tabxtablondon

6 Kuro Coffee ⚘

This little Japanese-inspired coffee shop is part of the Notting Hill Kuro massive, which includes Kuro Eatery two doors down (great for brunch) and Kuro Bakery that crafts the carby treats that pair with Kuro Coffee's high-end caffeinated offering.

3 Hillgate Street, Notting Hill, W8 7SP

kuro-london.com

7 Notting Hill Coffee Project

Clean lines and clean pours are the order of the day at this contemporary coffee shop. Pair your speciality brew with a pastry from the counter. In summer, check out the cold brew and menu of iced coffees, matcha, chai and turmeric.

63 Notting Hill Gate, W11 3JS

nottinghillcoffeeproject.com | ⊙ nottinghillcoffeeproject

8 LIFT ⚘

The uber-minimalist aesthetic at this speciality spot provides a blank canvas for the real star of the show: an ever-rotating curation of high-end beans from leading and international roasteries. Visit for espresso drinks, the pourover bar and hand-brewed coffee.

133 Kensington Church Street,
Kensington, W8 7LP

liftcoffeelondon.com | ⊙ liftcoffeelondon

9 Black Rabbit Cafe

Connection and community engagement are the name of the game at this indie on the Old Brompton Road. The Allpress house espresso is bolstered by a revolving line-up of guests on espresso and filter.

308 Old Brompton Road, SW5 9JF

blackrabbitcafe.co.uk | ⊙ blackrabbit_cafe

Boxcar Baker & Deli

(10) HJEM Kensington ⚇

A cool, clean and caffeinated slice of Danish fika in Kensington. This is a place to sip Climpson & Sons and Kiss the Hippo coffee – paired with a pastry – while revelling in calming vibes. Check out the sister site on Gloucester Road.

3 Launceston Place, South Kensington, W8 5RL

🅾 hjemkensington

(11) Guillam Coffee House ⚇

Spotlighting the distinct qualities and terroirs of single-origin coffees is the aim at these coffee houses in Kensington, Bayswater, Notting Hill and Mayfair. Each has a unique interior style inspired by the local neighbourhood.

24 Gloucester Road, South Kensington, SW7 4RB

guillam.co.uk | 🅾 guillamcoffeehouse

(12) Boxcar Baker & Deli ⚇

Marylebone's Boxcar Baker & Deli pairs its own-baked pastries, breads, salads, sarnies and wraps with a drinks list of wines, local craft beers, cocktails and, of course, speciality coffee. Pooches welcome too.

7a Wyndham Place, Marylebone, W1H 1PN

boxcar.co.uk | 🅾 boxcar_bakeranddeli

(13) Workshop Coffee

Visit the pioneering speciality roastery's central pit stop, just off Regent Street, for an espresso-based menu and fresh filters. Grab coffee to-go (although there's a small sit-in nook out back), quality carbs and fresh beans for your home hopper.

80a Mortimer Street, Fitzrovia, W1W 7FE

workshopcoffee.com | 🅾 workshopcoffee

(14) **Party at Pavilion**

253 Pavilion Road, Chelsea, SW1X 0BP

roastingparty.co.uk | 020 7730 6655

roastingparty

Don't be deterred from joining the queue at this popular Chelsea coffee shop; the line at Party at Pavilion moves quickly and everyone gets their two minutes of chat and connection with the talented baristas. Patience is rewarded with top-notch coffee that's been bronzed at the cafe's roastery HQ in Winchester.

Lured in by the Roasting Party beans, own-baked sweet and savoury carbs and freshly made sandwiches and salads, first-time Party-goers soon become regular returnees. The coffee is sweet and well balanced, forming the heart of an experience which the team strive to make easygoing and uplifting.

⚫ Seduced by the natural sweetness of Roasting Party beans? Buy a bag in-store

Connection is key, and the Party crew have been specially selected because they understand the powerful partnership between coffee and conversation and know how to build relationships – one flat white at a time.

Two house-roasted bean styles – one crafted for milk-based brews and another for black coffee – deliver a high-quality experience, so everyone leaves the shop with a great coffee in their hand and a smile on their face.

Established
2017

Key roaster
Roasting Party

Brewing method
Nitro, cold brew, batch filter

Machine
La Marzocco KB90

Grinder
Mahlkonig E80, Mahlkonig EK43

Opening hours
Mon-Fri
7.30am-5pm
Sat-Sun
9am-4pm

Kaffeine London

15 Kiss the Hippo
– Fitzrovia

Swing by the innovative and planet-friendly roastery's cafes – there are two in Fitzrovia plus others in Chelsea, Mayfair, King's Cross, Covent Garden, Shoreditch and Richmond – to sample its organic blends, single-origin brews and cafe food.

51 Margaret Street, Fitzrovia, W1W 8SG

kissthehippo.com | ⊙ kissthehippo

16 Qima Cafe

Elegant patisserie and ethically sourced coffee collide at this outpost devoted to decadence in Fitzrovia – the UK's first tree-to-cup cafe. Perfect pairings include the likes of velvety flat white (made from beans sourced directly from smallholder farmers) and a buttery pistachio croissant.

21 Warren Street, Fitzrovia, W1T 5LT

qimacafe.com | ⊙ qima.cafe

17 Saint Espresso
– Camden

The OG Saint Espresso outlet, this coffee shop set the Camden caffeine scene ablaze when it opened on the iconic high street in 2011. Visit to sample uber-fresh house-roasted beans and be sure to check out Saint Espresso's other sites in the city (the Kentish Town find deals in epic brunches).

20 Camden High Street, Camden, NW1 0JH

saintespresso.com | ⊙ saintespresso

18 Kaffeine London

Fitzrovia meets antipodean coffee culture at Kaffeine on Eastcastle Street and its sister site on Great Titchfield Street. Kaffeine was an early pioneer on London's speciality scene and stays engaged with its audience through banging brews and fortnightly latte-art classes.

15 Eastcastle Street, Fitzrovia, W1T 3AY

kaffeine.co.uk | ⊙ kaffeinelondon

Kitchen Coffee

42 Newman Street, Fitzrovia, W1T 1QD

sendcoffee.co.uk

kitchen_coffee_london

Kitchen Coffee in Fitzrovia is the newest addition to SEND Coffee's clutch of cafes, which operates alongside the company's speciality coffee roastery and training academy for young adults with additional needs. This latest outlet is the baby of the group and follows in the footsteps of its sibling cafes in delivering a next-level coffee experience crafted by trained-to-excellence baristas.

With multiple brewing methods available – including espresso, pourover, batch and cold brew – and a team equipped with in-depth knowledge of each own-roasted coffee, this is an ideal spot at which to dispense with the usual house-roast flat white order and go off-piste.

⚡ Ever tried cupping coffee? Ask the team for a taste of the flavour-profiling process

Like to chase your coffee with more coffee? After sampling the best of the SEND beans, ask what's on the exclusive off-menu list of guest roasts. The team procure the good stuff from roasteries they rate, including Dark Woods, The Barn and Takamura, so there's usually something interesting to try.

Check out other SEND cafes in Tandy Place, Cullum Street and Camden Road.

Established
2024

Key roaster
SEND Coffee

Brewing method
Espresso, batch brew, cold brew, pourover

Machine
Sanremo Café Racer

Grinder
Mahlkonig EK43,
Mahlkonig E80,
Mythos One

Opening hours
Mon-Fri
8am-4pm

Lavelle Bike + Bean

20 Caravan ⚭

There are plenty of Caravan cafes where you can revel in house-roasted coffee and global dishes from an all-day menu. Located in a Grade-II listed former grain store near King's Cross, this one has an industrial-cool vibe that complements its slick beany offering.

1 Granary Square, N1C 4AA

caravanandco.com | ⊙ caravanroastery

21 Store St Espresso ⚭

One of the early wave riders of London's speciality coffee scene, since 2010 Store St Espresso's flagship cafe has been a go-to spot for those looking to sink an elite brew crafted from Square Mile beans.

40 Store Street, Bloomsbury, WC1E 7DB

storestespresso.co.uk | ⊙ storestreetespresso

22 Omotesando Koffee ⚭

This is the London outlet of Eiichi Kunitomo's collection of cafes, which started in Tokyo. Visit for a super-zen coffee vibe as you perch at the pared-back brew bar.

8 Newman Street, Rathbone Square, Fitzrovia, W1T 1PB

ooo-koffee.com | ⊙ omotesando.koffee

23 Lavelle Bike + Bean

This centrally located spot, set on two levels, combines a coffee shop serving uber-healthy food with an e-bike and lifestyle store. Keep an eye out for regular wellness events with guest speakers.

51-52 Rathbone Place, W1T 1JP

lavellecoffee.com | ⊙ lavellecoffee

Söderberg

(24) **Söderberg** – Soho ✂

Visit Söderberg for a classic fika hit of Scandi coffee and cake – or, better, cinnamon and cardamom buns. This Swedish coffee shop and bakery is found amid the nonstop bustle of Berwick Street and has a 1960s-style lounge downstairs. Check out sister sites in Dulwich – and Edinburgh!

36 Berwick Street, Soho, W1F 8RR

soderberg.uk | 🅾 soderbergbakery

(25) **Café Leon Dore** ✂

Queen's, NY, converges with Soho by way of Greece at this coffee shop thanks to its old-school-aesthetic-meets-fashion vibes. Assembly Coffee beans are crafted into espresso drinks and the iconic iced freddo cappuccino on a menu inspired by Greek coffee-and-pastry culture.

32 Broadwick Street, Soho, W1F 8JB

eu.aimeleondore.com | 🅾 aimeleondore

(26) **flat white**

Keeping Soho expertly caffeinated via silky foam and syrupy espresso since the early noughties, this tiny Berwick Street stalwart is a no-brainer for a caffeine and sugar hit.

17 Berwick Street, Soho, W1F 0PT

flatwhitesoho.co.uk | 🅾 flatwhitesoho

(27) **Formative Coffee**

Founded by UK Barista Champion Ian Kissick, Formative is a magnet for coffee geeks looking to enjoy both the craft and science of speciality coffee. Uber-sleek minimalist surroundings let the coffee do the talking.

4 Butler Place, Westminster, SW1H 0RH

formative.coffee | 🅾 formativecoffee

(28) Iris & June – Victoria

1 Howick Place, Westminster, SW1P 1WG

irisandjune.com | 020 7828 3130

 Iris & June irisandjune

This central coffee shop is named after founder Jodie's grandmothers – those ladies who, when they weren't catching up over cuppas and cakes in a local coffee shop, taught Jodie to cook. Iris & June honours them in a menu of wholesome fodder and first-rate caffeine served in a buzzy environment.

A squad of cheery baristas serve Ozone-roasted beans in this bright space, mixing things up with a fortnightly rotation of two or three single-origin guest roasts.

Check out Iris & June's takeaway-only site at Holborn Circus

Daily changing lunch menus reflect the season but usually feature an assortment of mega salads and fluffy frittatas, while the selection of baked goods are switched up each week. Iris & June's signature dishes sell out quickly so visitors should pop in early if they want to get their chops around the popular cheese scones or buttermilk banana bread, both served with lashings of salted butter.

Rest assured, whether it's a salad of lentils, leaves, radish, medjool dates, toasted sesame seeds and spicy tahini or a slice of date and butterscotch cake, it will have been made from scratch in the kitchen that day.

Established
2014

Key roaster
Ozone
Coffee Roasters

Brewing method
Espresso, batch brew, V60, AeroPress, cold brew

Machine
La Marzocco
Linea PB

Grinder
Mahlkonig E80 GbW

Opening hours
Mon-Fri
7.30am-4.30pm

(29) **Nostos Coffee – St James's**

6 Orchard Place, St James's, SW1H 0BF

nostoscoffee.co.uk

nostoscoffee

Serving coffee with a scientific edge in the heart of St James's is the mission of Nostos Coffee's flagship store – a brother to the Battersea original.

Nostos translates from the ancient Greek of *The Odyssey* as "homecoming", which is apt at this venue that prides itself on being a welcoming place to enjoy exceptional coffee and service while catching up with friends.

More than just a coffee shop, Nostos is a coffee experience. Director and coffee innovator Edison Shehu explains: *'We are one of a select few in the UK to present an experience bar with a frozen-coffee menu. Our unique approach to pourover coffee utilises custom water recipes made with Apax Lab and Lotus Water minerals to deliver the best possible cup.'*

Keep an eye open for Nostos' popular collaborative cupping events

Nostos was also one of the first to launch freeze-distilled flat whites in a cafe setting. The concept was developed for coffee competitions, but anyone can experience it here. Other serve styles are showcased alongside, including Origami, AeroPress and batch filter – each designed with a different recipe for optimum results.

The attention to detail and care paid to crafting brews are standout. *'We take pride in being baristas and aim to change people's perceptions, so that being a barista is viewed as a profession and a career,'* says Edison.

Established
2021

Key roaster
Nostos Coffee

Brewing method
Espresso,
Origami dripper,
AeroPress,
batch brew

Machine
Victoria Arduino
Black Eagle Maverick,
Slayer Single Group

Grinder
Mahlkonig E80,
Titus Nautilus

Opening hours
Mon-Fri
7.30am-5pm
Sat
8.30am-5pm
Sun
9.30am-4.30pm

(30) Gramos Coffee Bar

Ice Cube 1 (Regent's Canal exit), King's Cross Underground Station, N1 9AP

gramoscoffee.com

gramoscoffee

© Distilled Stills

The morning commute becomes a positive joy when you can pick up a proper flat white on your way to the office.

Gramos is a boutique coffee bar – located one level down in King's Cross tube station – that works entirely with own-roasted beans. Expect single-origin coffees of exceptional quality as espressos are graded 85+ and filters 87+.

As a result, Gramos enjoys a loyal following of coffee lovers who appreciate the attention to detail given to how their brew tastes, looks and is prepared. For those just passing through, it's a very pleasant surprise to score caffeine of this quality at one of the capital's busiest stations.

🔵 Got a moment to stop? Check out the range of merch and home-brewing equipment

Regulars love that they're often served by owners Rodolfo and Charlotte, who are passionate about delivering excellent service. Even in rush hour the operation is slick and efficient but, if you've the time, it's worth sitting in to appreciate your flat white or V60 pourover while watching the station's hustle and bustle. In keeping with the quality-service ethos, customers aren't charged extra for oat milk, decaf (currently a washed sugar-cane process from Colombia) or low-caffeine options.

Want to replicate the experience in your own kitchen? Get Gramos-roasted beans delivered to your door via the online subscription service.

Established
2022

Key roaster
Gramos
Coffee Roasters

Brewing method
Espresso, batch filter, pourover

Machine
La Marzocco
Linea

Grinder
Mahlkonig E80 GbW,
Mahlkonig EK43,
Victoria Arduino
Mythos One

Opening hours
Mon-Fri
7am-7pm
Sat
8am-8pm
Sun
9am-5pm

Monmouth Coffee Company – Covent Garden

(31) 26 Grains

Inspired by the Danish way of life – and, in particular, Copenhagen's love of porridge – founder Alex Hely-Hutchinson and team have created a quality coffee and creative breakfast-leaning menu in the heart of Covent Garden.

1 Neal's Yard, Covent Garden, WC2H 9DP

26grains.com | © 26grains

(32) Monmouth Coffee Company – Covent Garden ⅋

Swing by this Covent Garden coffee shop to sample the pioneering roastery's well-crafted coffees, buy fresh beans and grab a locally made pastry. You'll have to be lucky (or early) to nab one of limited seats.

27 Monmouth Street, Covent Garden, WC2H 9EU

monmouthcoffee.co.uk | © monmouthcoffee

(33) Arôme Bakery ⅋

An eclectic fusion of French baking techniques and eastern ingredients results in unconventional homemade creations like miso-bacon escargot at this indie French-Asian bakery. Good eats are accompanied by quality coffee. Find a sister site on Duke Street.

9 Mercer Street, The Yards, Covent Garden, WC2H 9QJ

aromebakery.co.uk | © aromebakerylondon

(34) Redemption Roasters ⅋

Seek out this spacious urban oasis for a moment of calm caffeination in Covent Garden. Part of Redemption Roasters' mini-chain of speciality cafes in the city, this new outpost is a crowd-pleasing spot for brunch and brews.

40 Drury Lane, Covent Garden, WC2B 5RR

redemptionroasters.com | © redemptionroasters

(35) Drury 188-189

188-189 Drury Lane, Covent Garden, WC2B 5QD

drury188189.co.uk | 020 7831 7555

 drury188189 drury188189

Sweet and caffeinated thrills are the order of the day at this Covent Garden find.

From Monday to Sunday, the walk-ins-only cafe churns out lip-smackingly smooth Allpress brews and a delicious bill of brunch dishes which includes its signature serve: french toast. The fluffy ensemble comes in various guises, including soft brioche bread topped with seasonal fruits, greek yogurt, organic raspberry jam, pistachios and a generous dusting of cinnamon sugar.

Close friends and founders Cemal and Ali established Drury 188-189 to be a cosy spot for soul-nourishing escapism. Unlike so many fast-paced and monotone-vibe city cafes, this is an inviting place where likeminded folk can engage with great food, coffee and chat. The lack of wifi encourages guests to interact, while the stack of books is ideal for those who prefer to hunker down solo.

🌀 Add to the extensive collection of napkin art that decorates the walls – they've been created by customers from all over the world

Sweet and savoury pancakes have recently been added to the menu and are so delicious they're rivalling the french toast for top-dog status. Nutritious salads and classic cafe fare such as eggs benny and avo on sourdough also feature on the line-up.

Established
2016

Key roaster
Allpress Espresso

Brewing method
Espresso, filter

Machine
La Marzocco
Linea PB

Grinder
Victoria Arduino
Mythos One

Opening hours
Mon-Fri
7.30am-5pm
Sat-Sun
8am-6pm

36 News & Coffee ⅋

A contender for London's most unusual speciality coffee experience, these coffee newsstands dole out stimulating caffeination and hand-picked publications in equal measure. Find one at Chalk Farm, another outside Holborn Station and more in Barcelona, Madrid and Valencia.

Holborn Station, Kingsway Newsstand, WC2B 6AA

newsandcoffee.eu | ⓘ newsandcoffee.eu

37 Meletius Speciality Coffee Roasters

Bubblegum-pink interiors and a neon sign suggesting customers 'spread the love' hint at the feelgood energy in this cafe from roastery Meletius. Enjoy the flavour-packed blends from one of the plush pink sofas.

37-39 High Holborn, WC1V 6AA

meletius.com | ⓘ meletiuscoffee

38 Prufrock Coffee

Founded by three bona fide coffee lovers, Prufrock is a great place to dive into the world of speciality coffee. Explore the ever-changing coffee menu, peruse pro brewing gear and maybe even undertake a barista course.

23-25 Leather Lane, EC1N 7TE

prufrockcoffee.com | ⓘ prufrockcoffee

39 Devotion Coffee ⅋

For its sites in Islington and Clerkenwell, family-run Devotion sources heaps of interesting and unusual guest coffees that merit numerous return visits. They've even garnered devotion from fans such as Keira Knightley and Jack O'Connell.

55-57 Rosebery Avenue, Clerkenwell, EC1R 4SD

ⓘ devotion_coffee

⓸⓪ Colonna & Small's

96a Leather Lane, EC1N 7TX

colonnacoffee.com

⬛ colonnacoffee ⭕ colonnacoffee

Following months of caffeine-jitter-levels of anticipation from Colonna's speciality followers, its Leather Lane outpost opened in September 2023 to immediate fanfare.

The coffee shop is the second Colonna & Small's outpost created by three-time UK Barista Champion Maxwell Colonna-Dashwood. He launched his original shop in 2009 in Bath, which became a pioneer of the UK's speciality movement. Famed for its use of high-scoring coffees from indie roasteries, slick serves and cutting-edge innovation, the spot received the Best Coffee Shop in Europe title in 2016.

🔵 Explore the menu of frozen exclusive and limited-release coffees

In 2015, the team began roasting beans of exceptional quality, which visitors can roadtest alongside fellow enthusiasts in this London spot. 'Our coffee shops are dedicated spaces to showcase the most unique and exceptional cup profiles, and ignite conversations surrounding coffee,' says Maxwell. 'We aim to share our passion with likeminded individuals, offer a personalised experience and encourage exploration of new coffees while ensuring recommendations are tailored.'

Visit to lose yourself in the world of gilt-edged brewing, served with a warm welcome.

Established
2023

Key roaster
Colonna Coffee

Brewing method
Espresso, AeroPress

Machine
La Marzocco
Linea PB

Grinder
Mahlkonig EK43

Opening hours
Mon, Fri
8am-4pm
Tue-Thu
7.30am-4pm
Sat
9am-4pm
Sun
10am-4pm

© Lauren Kallen

Rosslyn – Queen Victoria Street

(41) Iris & June
– Holborn Circus %

Find this bijou outpost of Iris & June's Victoria HQ opposite the historical church of St Andrew Holborn. Service is takeaway-only, so swing by to grab an Ozone coffee and a fresh carby treat to-go.

1a Holborn Circus, EC1N 2HB
irisandjune.com | 🔘 irisandjune

(42) Pickwick Coffee Club %

This coffee shop honours its historic journalistic setting with well-crafted Workshop-roasted coffee plus pastries from Rockstar Bakers. Pull up a pew and scroll the news while sipping a house long black or guest filter.

110 Fleet Street, EC4A 2AF
🔘 pickwickcoffeeclub

(43) Rosslyn
– Queen Victoria Street %

Rosslyn is a sleek find for carefully crafted brews made using Origin Coffee beans. Swing by – once the traders have downed their caffeine hit and are at their desks – to enjoy a quiet moment with a flawless flat white and buttery pastry. Find sister City sites at London Wall and Tower 42.

78 Queen Victoria Street, EC4N 4SJ
rosslyncoffee.com | 🔘 rosslyncoffee

(44) Ozone Coffee
– Shoreditch %

New Zealand's Ozone was one of the first to showcase speciality in London via its roastery and cafes, and this Shoreditch stalwart remains an on-point spot to sample own-roasted beans in brews. Pair your flat white with a topped flatbread or the house spesh: banana bread with smoked butter.

11 Leonard Street, Shoreditch, EC2A 4AQ
ozonecoffee.co.uk | 🔘 ozonecoffeeuk

(45) Party at Moorgate

71 Moorgate, EC2R 6BH

roastingparty.co.uk | 020 7730 6655

roastingparty

Party at Moorgate, with its unmissable stripy awning, is a welcome sight amid the hubbub of the City. Given the setting of this outpost of the Roasting Party family, most Party-goers in this neck of the woods are in perpetual motion, ricocheting through the door to grab a quick caffeine hit and a Roasting Party-made bakery treat, salad or sarnie.

However, if there's space on the bench seating, customers can take a pause from the daily grind to watch the expert baristas work with own-roasted beans and appreciate the care that goes into crafting one of life's little pleasures.

Two roasting programmes – one for milk-based coffees and another for black – from the house roastery provide the team with all the goods required to create deliciously sweet coffee, every which way.

Want to hone your at-home coffee skills? Check out Roasting Party's BrewTube

No matter how fleeting the exchange, the Party team like to make sure the visit is memorable, so coffee's always served with a smile and friendly chat. Swing by to say hi and experience the easygoing expertise that's the Roasting Party MO.

Established
2018

Key roaster
Roasting Party

Brewing method
Cold brew,
batch filter

Machine
La Marzocco
Linea PB

Grinder
Mahlkonig E80,
Mahlkonig EK43

Opening hours
Mon-Thu
7am-4pm
Fri
7am-1.30pm

(46) Curators Coffee

9a Cullum Street, EC3M 7JJ

sendcoffee.co.uk

curators_coffee

This multi-award-winning cafe on the corner of Cullum Street is a great find for a feelgood hit in the City.

It's been created by the team that runs SEND Coffee roastery and training school, so visitors are guaranteed silky flat whites and fruity batch brews powered by drum-fresh beans. Yet, alongside their own-roasted SEND beans, the crew supplement with rare and interesting guest roasts, keeping customers surprised and delighted.

🌀 Batch brew is the speciality – the team sell roughly 20 litres of the liquid gold each day

Although Curator's story began in 2010 as a barista-led organisation that aimed to spread the joy of speciality, its most inspiring chapter opened in 2020 when the team started a charity project to train young adults with disabilities and help them move into careers in coffee.

Over the years, the crew have scooped numerous accolades for their social enterprises and coffee skills: La Marzocco Barista Hero, UKBC, UK Coffee Roasters Championships, Mayor of London Adult Learning Awards, Queen's Awards for Enterprise, plus an Outstanding rating from Ofsted.

More recently, the Curators team learnt British Sign Language (BSL) to better communicate with one of their baristas. This led to a new initiative: order in BSL and bag a free brew.

Established
2010

Key roaster
SEND Coffee

Brewing method
Espresso, batch brew, cold brew

Machine
Sanremo Café Racer, Victoria Arduino Eagle One

Grinder
Mahlkonig EK43, Mahlkonig E80, Victoria Arduino Mythos One

Opening hours
Mon-Fri
7.30am-4pm

(47) Three Wheels Coffee

Unit 312, The Retail Arcade, 32 London Bridge Street, SE1 9SG

threewheelscoffee.com

f threewheelscoffee threewheelscoffee

Over ten years ago, Rory Doyle engineered a 70kg coffee machine onto a tricycle to make his own espresso bar on wheels. The idea came from his travels in South America, where he'd been bowled over by the vibrant coffee culture. He returned home, inspired to introduce a slice of it to a London audience.

While the Three Wheels set-up has evolved (it's now an espresso bar in The Retail Arcade adjacent to London Bridge station), Rory's focus on quality coffee has remained constant.

Less cafe, more coffee station, Three Wheels is all about speedy service, high-grade caffeine and a rock-up-order-and-go vibe that flows as smoothly as the shots streaming from the La Marzocco. The bar is unique in that it's completely open with no counter, so customers are amid the action as their drinks are being made.

🔋 Early morning commute? Check out the fresh juices and breakfast bowls

Since he launched Three Wheels, Rory has worked with Volcano Coffee Works and Assembly, the latter continuing to deliver the house espresso. Guest filters also feature for batch brews and alternative espresso-based pours.

Established
2013

Key roaster
Assembly Coffee

Brewing method
Espresso,
batch brew

Machine
La Marzocco
Linea PB

Grinder
Mazzer Robur S,
Mazzer Major,
Mahlkonig Tanzania

Opening hours
Mon-Fri
7am-3.30pm

48 Rosslyn – London Wall ⚬⚬

Combining founders' Mat Russell and James Hennebry's Australian and Irish heritages, this cafe (one of a trio) fuses the coffee creds and style of an antipodean cafe with the warmth and hospitality of an Irish pub.

118 London Wall, EC2Y 5JA

rosslyncoffee.com | ⓘ rosslyncoffee

49 Saint Nine Coffee

This pint-size addition to the Southwark speciality scene houses eight coveted window seats and is just a short walk from Tate Modern. Visit for ultra-slick serves beneath a neck-craning mural that climbs up the wall and across the ceiling.

67 Southwark Street, Southwark, SE1 0HX

ⓘ saintninecoffee

Latana

Monmouth Coffee Company – The Borough

50 Lantana ⚬⚬

Lantana prides itself on being a little slice of Australia in London. Experience it at this London Bridge cafe and its sister sites in Fitzrovia and Shoreditch. A menu of quality food is served all day – brunch being a speciality – along with coffee roasted by Climpson & Sons.

44-46 Southwark Street, SE1 1UN

lantana.co.uk | ⓘ lantanalondon

51 Monmouth Coffee Company – The Borough ⚬⚬

The stalwart roastery's Borough shop deals in syrupy espressos and perfectly crafted pourovers, plus an exciting selection of fresh beans and coffee gear to get your own brewing on point.

2 Park Street, The Borough, SE1 9AB

monmouthcoffee.co.uk | ⓘ monmouthcoffee

52 Frequency ⚬⚬

Developed by the passion of their owner Justo, multi-concept Frequency has five outposts and incorporates a roasting operation, espresso bars, delicious food and workspaces. Hunt them out in King's Cross, Angel, Paddington, Millenium Bridge and Bermondsey.

157 Tower Bridge Road, Bermondsey, SE1 3LW

frequencycoffee.com | ⓘ frequency.london

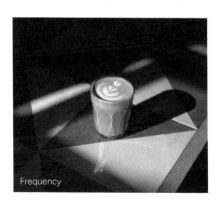

Frequency

(53) Big Bro Espresso

bigbroespresso.com

 bigbroespresso bigbroespresso

Big Bro founder Marc Radville is in possession of exactly what's required to make this business a success – in his words: *'Wheels and OCD about espresso'*.

Marc fell in love with the speciality coffee scene while travelling in New Zealand, and on his return to the UK honed his barista skills in busy London coffee shops while setting up his own business. He's now the proud owner of two coffee vehicles – a vintage Citroën van and a horsebox with a Linea PB apiece – and works alongside his team of enthusiastic baristas to take speciality coffee to the people.

☕ Up for freshly baked Viennoiserie? Get your pastry fix at Big Bro, too

Although Big Bro specialises in providing the coffee for film and TV sets, punters can get a slice of the action via private hire for events or by following Big Bro on Insta and tracking them down wherever they're located that day. They've rocked up everywhere from Covent Garden and Blackheath to Canary Wharf, Peckham, Lewisham and Wimbledon ...

The Big Bro team believe in doing things well, and have a custom roast created for them by London roastery Code.194. In an interesting plot twist, the roastery was co-founded by Dumo Mathema, an old school friend of Marc's own big bro, Paul.

Established
2015

Key roaster
Code.194
Coffee Roasters

Brewing method
Espresso, filter

Machine
La Marzocco
Linea PB

Grinder
Mahlkonig E80S,
Mahlkonig EK43 S

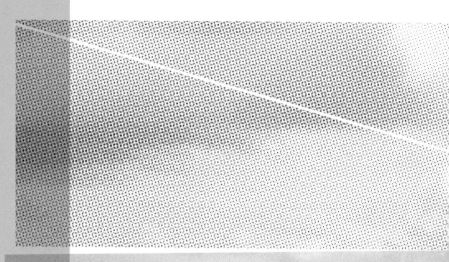

North London cafes

Locations are approximate

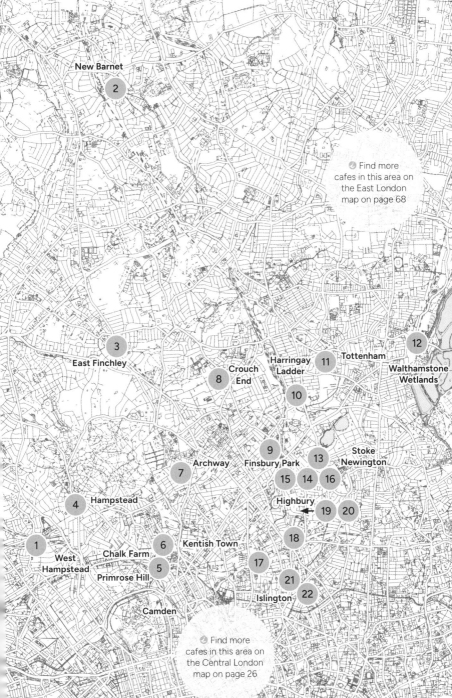

New Barnet

2

🍃 Find more
cafes in this area on
the East London
map on page 68

12

3

East Finchley

Harringay
Ladder

11

Tottenham

Crouch
End

8

Walthamstone
Wetlands

10

9

13

Stoke
Newington

7

Archway

Finsbury Park

15 **14** **16**

4

Hampstead

Highbury ←

19 **20**

1

6

Kentish Town

18

West
Hampstead

Chalk Farm

5

17

Primrose Hill

21

Islington

22

Camden

🍃 Find more
cafes in this area on
the Central London
map on page 26

53

(1) intermission

Unit 2 , The Hardy Building, Heritage Lane, West Hampstead, NW6 2BR

intermission.coffee

🔲 intermission.coffee

This caffeinated oasis in West Hampstead is an ideal place at which to press pause on the daily grind. Each morning a queue streams from its doors as locals wait their turn to get their intermission fix of oat flat white and homemade banana bread, plus a bag of own-roasted beans to continue the coffee thrills at home.

While some coffee shops treat filter brews as second tier, at intermission it's the focus. The team ensure the method delivers results that are just as showstopping as the espresso-based classics. The pop-green brew bar is the best place to sample meticulously prepared filter coffees that celebrate the journey of coffee – from cherry to cup. It's where the baristas employ a range of equipment, exacting standards and flavour-popping beans to take visitors Down The Rabbit Hole (one of intermission's must-try coffees, FYI).

🔵 Visit on a Saturday to pair your pick with a homemade cardamom bun

Intermission's commitment to supporting people and planet begins with the farmers at origin and the coffee cherries they produce. Through the roastery-cafe's 5p-per-cup scheme, every cup of coffee purchased supports coffee-growing communities facing environmental and socio-political hardship.

The friendly baristas are always keen to share the stories behind the beans, revealing more about their unique flavours and, most importantly, the people who grew them.

Established
2020

Key roaster
intermission

Brewing method
Espresso, Orea, cold brew, filter

Machine
Mavam MACH 2

Grinder
Mahlkonig E65S GbW, Mythos One, Mahlkonig EK43

Opening hours
Mon-Fri
7am-4pm
Sat
8am-5pm
Sun
9am-4pm

(2) Old Bank Coffee House

253 East Barnet Road, Barnet, EN4 8ST

oldbankcoffeehouse.co.uk

oldbankcoffeehouse oldbankcoffeebarnet

The folk of East Barnet Village rejoiced when this former bank received a glow-up and reopened as a family-owned coffee house paying out good vibes, good coffee and good company.

'Come and sit with us; no rush, no reservations' is the team's mantra, which is testament to the warm welcome served up in this light-filled space. The all-female team proclaim this isn't a bog-standard coffee spot; it's more a destination where consistently stellar drinks are served with a side of daily-made artisan bakes and toasties (courtesy of award-winning Holtwhites Bakery). This approach has seen the venue draw in loyal regulars along with an eclectic mix of visiting coffee sippers from near and far. It's not an unusual sight to see WFHers sharing table space with emergency service workers, dog walkers and parent groups (the cafe also has a secluded play space and pram area).

🔵 The team have introduced a rotating guest roaster programme to bring their favourite coffees to East Barnet

The house beans come from pioneering East London roastery Climpson & Sons. Try them in an espresso drink such as a flat white with quirky latte art, or opt for a filter brew to experience seasonal single origins from across the globe, which are switched up regularly.

Established
2022

Key roaster
Climpson & Sons

Brewing method
Espresso,
filter, V60, cold brew

Machine
Conti MC Ultima

Grinder
Mahlkonig E65S

Opening hours
Mon-Fri
8am-4pm
Sat-Sun
9am-3pm

(3) Campbell & Syme Coffee Roasters

9 Fortis Green, East Finchley, N2 9JR

campbellandsyme.co.uk

f campbellandsyme campbellandsyme

The Campbell & Syme tribe believe *'outstanding coffee does not just appear'*. They're all about celebrating the collective effort made by every hardworking human who contributes on the journey from bean to cup: from the smallholders who grow the cherries to the coffee lovers who get to sip the prepared brews.

The team's link in this coffee chain began in 2012 with the launch of their coffee shop in East Finchley. It became the spot where the C&S roastery operations eventually began, before the team outgrew the space and relocated to Kings Langley in Hertfordshire.

⏱ Book one of the cupping sessions to sample the team's latest seasonal finds

These days, this original location specialises in serving own-roasted filter and espresso drinks (there are usually two single-origin espressos and three different filter coffees – two hand-poured and one batch brew – to choose from). It's also where home brewers can pick up beans and equipment. A small menu sees the caffeine matched with seasonal toasties, open sarnies, granola and house-baked goods. Toasted banana bread with butter and the guac on sourdough open sandwich are house faves.

The community vibe is nurtured by the village atmosphere of this friendly north London neighbourhood. Customers drop in to connect (with each other rather than their inbox, thanks to a laptop ban), drink good coffee and enjoy lively conversation with knowledgeable baristas.

Established
2012

Key roaster
Campbell & Syme
Coffee Roasters

Brewing method
Espresso, batch brew,
V60, filter

Machine
Conti MC Ultima 2

Grinder
Compak F8-DBW

Opening hours
Mon-Fri
8am-3pm
Sat
9am-4pm

(4) Hagen ⚭

This collection of Danish espresso bars is spread across London, delivering Copenhagen-style fika moments. Swing by to sink a quality speciality coffee from an array of global roasteries, paired with sweet sustenance.

70 Hampstead High Street, Hampstead, NW3 1QP

thehagenproject.com | ⊙ thehagenproject

(5) Luminary Bakery ⚭

This social enterprise uses the power of baking as a tool to empower disadvantaged women and take them on a journey through entrepreneurship. Feel the love at this Camden cafe and bakery and sister outlet on Allen Road in Stoke Newington.

47 Chalk Farm Road, Camden, NW1 8AJ

luminarybakery.com | ⊙ luminarybakery

(6) The Fields Beneath

You'd be hard pressed to find another place in Kentish Town that pours the same amount of love into crafting a quality brew. The team source beans directly from a friend in Costa Rica, which are roasted by Butterworth & Son and served alongside plant-based eats.

52a Prince of Wales Road,
Kentish Town West, NW5 3LN

thefieldsbeneath.com | ⊙ fieldsbeneath

(7) Cricks Corner

This cornerstone of the Archway community serves up cheerful neighbourhood vibes with its top-notch coffees, keeping its regulars expertly caffeinated and smiling. Check out the range of retail beans for home brewing.

Dartmouth Park Hill, Archway, 80 N19 5HU

crickscorner.co.uk | ⊙ crickscorner

⑧ **Velasquez & van Wezel**

78 Park Road, Crouch End, N8 8JQ

velasquezandvanwezel.co.uk | 07930 480160

📷 velasquez_vanwezel

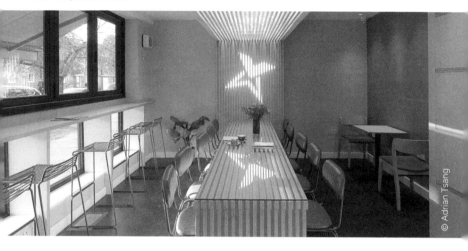

© Adrian Tsang

Traceability – from seed to cup – is the raison d'être at Crouch End's slick coffee bar Velasquez & van Wezel. Named after its Dutch and Colombian founders, this is a space to sample world-class coffee and get involved in caffeinated events.

The duo opened their coffee bar in 2016, after discovering a mutual love of the perfect brew. Coffee flows through both their upbringings: Colombian-born Oscar was raised on a farm in the Andes highlands, east of Bogota, where beans are grown and roasted. Over 5,000 miles away in a small town in the east Netherlands, Martin grew up with his grandad selling loose coffee beans out of large tins in the family corner shop. Fuelled by nostalgia, respect for the industry seeps through everything they do.

🔵 Book a place on one of the monthly cupping sessions

With main roaster duties covered by London's Square Mile and Amsterdam institution Friedhats, guest spots are filled by international finds from Rotterdam roasters Manhattan and Schot, Barcelona's Nomad and Amsterdam's Uncommon, among others.

Roll up and try one of the new serving flights showcasing the best V&vW has on offer. Consisting of a guest espresso, a guest piccolo and a guest filter coffee, it's a feast for the senses.

Established
2016

Key roaster
Square Mile
Coffee Roasters,
Friedhats Coffee
Roasters

Brewing method
Espresso,
batch filter

Machine
Kees van der
Westen Spirit

Grinder
Mahlkonig EK,
Mahlkonig E80,
Mahlkonig E65,
Victoria Arduino
Mythos One

Opening hours
Mon-Fri
7am-4pm
Sat-Sun
8am-4pm

9 Common Ground

Switch the inbox for IRL interactions at this relaxed, laptop-free space. Globally inspired (and meat/fish-free) food is bolstered by a quality collection of cocktails and juices. Sunny day? Take your Dark Arts coffee out onto the plant-packed terrace.

49 Stroud Green Road, near Finsbury Park, N4 3EF

commongroundlondon.co.uk

⊙ commongroundlondon

11 Perkyn's

This N15 neighbourhood coffee shop delivers the full package, complementing its quality coffee offering with great food, craft beers, natural wines, poetry workshops, creative sessions and open-mic comedy nights.

10 Vicarage Parade, West Green Road, Tottenham, N15 3BL

perkyns.square.site | ⊙ perkynsn15

10 The Dusty Knuckle ✗

The purpose of this esteemed cafe-bakery isn't just to feed patrons with droolworthy bakes and brews but also to do good in the community. Its youth programme offers training, mentorship and employment to at-risk young people. Hit this Harringay Ladder cafe but also discover more Dusty Knuckle deliciousness in Dalston.

429 Green Lanes, Harringay Ladder, N4 1HA

thedustyknuckle.com | ⊙ thedustyknuckle

12 Table13

Drawing on life's greatest pleasures (coffee, bread and wine – duh) this vibrant cafe, bakery and bar positions its daytime offering around Wood St Coffee and house-baked sourdough. Come evening, it switches things up with small plates and speciality wine.

Hale Village, Waterside Way, N17 9FU

table13london.com | ⊙ table13_london

(13) Brewed Online

263 Green Lanes, Stoke Newington, N4 2UX

brewed.online

 brewed.online brewed.online

Here's a novel approach to serving speciality coffee: become an online hub for the best British-roasted beans then stock your cafe with a bean offering to match your busy online store. That's how it works at Brewed. *'I think we probably stock the largest number of retail beans of any shop in the country,'* says co-founder Robert Sharples. *'What's more, we sell them in enough volume that they're always fresh.'*

The Brewed team are adamant that every coffee lover deserves access to the very best, and they carefully fulfil all orders from the north London coffee shop.

🔵 Gain access to mates rates by becoming a Brewed Member

Alongside beans from the UK's best indie roasteries, visitors will find coffee equipment to suit numerous brew styles.

On the cafe front, Brewed serves exceptional espresso and filter coffee. Campbell & Syme is the main roastery on the menu, which is praise indeed from a business that carries up to 60 different roasts on its shelves. Every month, Brewed also hosts a shop takeover in collaboration with one of the 30+ roasteries they work with – think Old Spike, Hard Lines and Round Hill – and showcase their beans on guest and batch for the month.

Established
2018

Key roaster
Campbell & Syme

Brewing method
Espresso,
batch filter

Machine
Victoria Arduino
Eagle One

Grinder
Mahlkonig EK43,
Victoria Arduino
Mythos One,
Compak PKF × 2

Opening hours
Mon-Fri
8am-3.30pm
Sat-Sun
9am-5pm

(14) Fink's Salt & Sweet

70 Mountgrove Road, Highbury, N5 2LT

finks.co.uk

finks.london

Fink's Salt & Sweet is the proudly queer-owned indie chain's original (and largest) cafe, which celebrates a decade in Highbury.

This business has seen a number of incarnations: deli, dine-in brunch spot, restaurant, lifestyle and pantry store but, after a refurb in early 2024, now serves the discerning foodies of north London with on-point coffee and delicious cafe food. A small amount of indoor and outdoor seating is bolstered by a beautifully curated retail offering — with much of what's available on the shelves produced within walking distance.

🕑 Try a chicken caesar sandwich — it's earned a cult following

Owners Jess and Mat make pretty much all the edibles from scratch, from the unrivalled, chunkiest stacked sandwiches you've ever sunk your teeth into to hearty salads and lip-smacking desserts. The team also offer a catering service and have an arm specialising in the production of beautiful celebration cakes.

The coffee is equally as considered, with an obsessive attention to detail given to the espresso and filter brews made using Facility Blend and Villamaria Sugercane Decaf beans from Scenery Coffee Roasters.

Service is super friendly too; one visit to Fink's and you feel like family.

Established
2014

Key roaster
Scenery Coffee Roasters

Brewing method
Espresso, filter

Machine
Victoria Arduino Eagle One

Grinder
Mazzer Robur

Opening hours
Mon-Sat
8am-4pm
Sun
9am-4pm

15 Fink's – Gillespie

Swing by this compact coffee shop for its short-but-sweet breakfast and lunch menu and quality coffee, care of Caravan. Dusty Knuckle provides the bread while cakes, bakes and other edibles are all prepped in-house. Eat in or pick up to-go.

88 Gillespie Road, Finsbury Park, N5 1LN

finks.co.uk | ⊙ finks.london

16 Fink's – Pump House

Find this Fink's outpost at the Green Lanes entrance to Clissold Park. Four-legged friends are welcome – it even serves dog treats – making the daily trot around the park 100 per cent more appealing. Fuel your walk with Caravan coffee and a freshly made sarnie, cake or bake.

The Pump House, Clissold Park, N16 9DJ

finks.co.uk | ⊙ finks.london

17 Southpaw Coffee

Everything about Southpaw screams good taste. Oxford's Route Coffee drives the coffee menu, knockout bakes line the counter and shelves are stacked with a curation of vinyl, interesting wines and craft beers.

2 Roman Way, N7 8XG

southpawcoffee.co.uk | ⊙ southpawcoffeelondon

18 Kissa Wa

Highbury's Japanese cafe pairs Monmouth-roasted brews with a menu of Japanese breakfasts, lunches and homemade cakes and bakes. Grab a perch in the minimalist setting and soak up the relaxing atmosphere. Note: Kissa Wa is open Wednesday to Saturday.

15 Corsica Street, Highbury, N5 1JT

⊙ kissa_wa_cafe

(19) Saltine

11 Highbury Park, N5 1QJ

saltine.co.uk | 020 7916 0949

saltine.london

Mat Appleton and Jess Blackstone, the duo behind coffee favourite Fink's, launched this modern European restaurant with head chef Phil Wood (previously of Somerset House's Spring and St John Marylebone) in 2023.

The neighbourhood restaurant is found in Fink's home stomping ground, serving up food that's seasonal and contemporary. The menu includes the likes of pumpkin scapece with roasted hazelnuts and Spenwood cheese, mains of braised mutton with carrots and caraway, and puds like sticky toffee apple cake. The environment is dressed for dinner but Fink's playfulness is woven through the experience, alongside sustainability and provenance.

☕ Pastries come from Harringay and Dalston's finest, Dusty Knuckle

Unlike so many restaurants where the coffee is an afterthought, here it takes a starring role in a new coffee and cocktail bar that's situated up front. Scenery Coffee Roasters provides the beans and its Facility blend is the house choice for espresso drinks (which can also be taken to-go).

Coffee and a light food offering runs in the bar until the full menu kicks in at dinnertime, complemented by low-intervention wines, kitchen-led cocktails and quality post-dinner caffeination.

Established
2023

Key roaster
Scenery Coffee Roasters

Brewing method
Espresso, filter

Machine
Victoria Arduino Eagle One

Grinder
Mazzer Robur

Opening hours
Wed-Fri
5pm-11pm
Sat-Sun
9am-11pm

1b Highbury Park, N5 1QJ

profilecoffeen5.co.uk

profile.coffeen5

Profile Coffee is a peachy place to enjoy exceptional coffee. Natural tones, warming colour and modern decor combine to create a calm oasis in which to slow down and sip. The pace is different here, and that's what sets Profile apart from the crowd. Batch and hand brews are the order of the day, the team savouring the process in order to deliver a delicious and ritualistic coffee experience.

Sample the nitro matcha tonic made with Lalani & Co tea and Square Root fizz

Bean varietal, process and origin shine through in each serve. Profile founder Hugo James says: *'Highlighting these nuances is a role we take very seriously and with much pride.'*

La Cabra Coffee Roasters supplies the house beans, a Danish outfit focused on transparently sourcing coffees from quality farms. They create clean, bright coffees, without filter or espresso specifically in mind, which aligns well with Profile's mission to serve expressive drinks which leave a lasting impression.

You'll occasionally find guest roasteries Standout Coffee, Special Guests and Three Marks on the menu too – all companies that take the kind of holistic approach championed by Profile.

Established
2023

Key roaster
La Cabra
Coffee Roasters

Brewing method
Moccamaster,
Orea Brewer

Machine
Victoria Arduino
Eagle One 2AV

Grinder
Mahlkonig E65S × 2

Opening hours
Mon-Sun
8am-4pm

Pophams

(21) **High Ground**

Islington's pint-size speciality coffee and wine mash-up serves drinks of distinction alongside a counter of delicious pastries, cakes and sandwiches. Visit for coffee by day and wine and bevvies by night.

286 Upper Street, Islington, N1 2TZ

(○) highgroundn1

(22) **Pophams** ⚇

This stylish bakery-cafe in Islington deals in perfect pours and exceptional pastries. Visit for the flat whites and perfectly laminated treats, then pop next door to swoon over homewares at Pophams Home. Sister sites are found in London Fields and Victoria Park.

19 Prebend Street, Islington, N1 8PF

pophamsbakery.com | (○) pophamsbakery

East London cafes

1 Batch Baby
2 Commons
3 Friends of Ours
4 Origin Coffee Roasters
5 The Common E2
6 Esters
7 Brunswick East
8 Lodestar Coffee
9 e5 Bakehouse
10 215 Hackney Cafe
11 The Beehive
12 Paradox Design + Coffee
13 Ozone Coffee – London Fields
14 FORNO
15 Mae + Harvey
16 Fink's Chats
17 Clarnico Club
18 Back to Ours
19 Nagare Coffee
20 Potter & Reid
21 TRADE
22 Grove Lane Deli
23 Mouse Tail Coffee
24 640East
25 Ideal Espresso
26 Söderberg – East Dulwich
27 Nola Coffee
28 Good as Gold
29 Oscar's SE13
30 Servesmiths
31 Four Boroughs

Locations are approximate

Bushwood

Stoke Newington 10

6

Lower Clapton

8 16

7

Dalston Hackney

Hackney Wick

17

1 9

12 13 14

Bethnal Green

15 Bow

3 5 11

2

4

Shoreditch

Spitalfields 19 20 21

Canary Wharf

24

23

Rotherhithe

Greenwich

Deptford 25

Camberwell

22

Peckham

27

Brockley

28 Lewisham

26 East Dulwich

29

Find more
cafes in this area on
the South London
map on page 88

30

Catford

Crystal Palace

31

① Batch Baby

43 De Beauvoir Road, The Rose Lipman Building, N1 5SF

batchbaby.co.uk

☺ batchbabycoffee

When a cafe's customer base is mainly made up of baristas, it's a safe bet that the calibre of the caffeine is exceptional.

Batch Baby owners Saskia and Tom have spent more than a decade in the speciality industry and are incredibly passionate about quality coffee, only sourcing beans that tick the following boxes: uber high-end, of superlative quality or wildly intriguing.

Rather than sticking to one house roastery, they work with different roasteries from across the UK and showcase as many indie finds as possible each month – with the occasional special release from a far-flung roastery for good measure. The carefully selected beans are painstakingly brewed as espresso or filter to best highlight their unique profiles and tasting notes.

☕ With coffee this good, don't rush. Take your time to savour the unique experience

Created as a welcoming space where baristas and enthusiasts can fully indulge their passion for speciality coffee, Batch Baby is also the home of regular caffeine-related events and has one of Europe's largest and most varied coffee retail selections. It's the place to source a bag of high-grade or competition coffee at a surprisingly affordable price to take your home brewing next level.

Established
2021

Key roaster
Multiple roasteries

Brewing method
Espresso,
batch brew,
cold brew,
Orea

Machine
La Marzocco
KB90

Grinder
Mahlkonig EK43,
Mahlkonig E65S,
Victoria Arduino
Mythos One

Opening hours
Mon-Fri
7.30am-5pm
Sat
8am-5pm
Sun
9am-4pm

Commons

② **Commons** ༄

Linger at the flagship Old Street Works shop or get a caffeine hit on-the-go at Cannon Street for a kaleidoscope of coffees that champion bold flavours, under-explored regions and innovative techniques. Ceremonial-grade matcha and traditional chai bolster the experience.

207 City Road, EC1V 1JT

⬚ commonsldn

③ **Friends of Ours**

This award-winning brunch and speciality coffee find is a champion of fellow indie businesses and supporter of the local community. The menu is globally inspired and paired with quality brews, natural wines, craft beers and cocktails. Look out for pop-ups and collaborations.

61 Pitfield Street, N1 6BU

friendsofourscafe.com | ⬚ thefriendsofours

④ **Origin Coffee Roasters** ༄

The pioneering Cornish coffee brand's flagship site in Shoreditch showcases its own-roasted speciality beans at a brew bar that delivers monthly changing flavours in precision pours. Check out the B Corp's sister sites at Southwark and The British Library too.

65 Charlotte Road, Shoreditch, EC2A 3PE

origincoffee.co.uk | ⬚ origincoffeeroasters

⑤ **The Common E2**

There are dynamic cafes and then there are cafe/architecture design studio/art gallery/co-working-space hybrids like this find in Bethnal Green. Soak up the creative vibes while getting stuck into The Roasting Party coffee and a banging brunch.

53 Old Bethnal Green Road, Bethnal Green, E2 6QA

thecommone2.com | ⬚ thecommone2

6 Esters

These breakfast and lunch maestros craft creative dishes from scratch, based on quality produce from farmers in the home counties and East London. Pair the eats with espresso and filter brews made with beans from roasteries such as Ozone.

55 Kynaston Road, Stoke Newington, N16 0EB

estersn16.com | ⓘ estersn16

7 Brunswick East ⠹

This off-the-beaten-track brunch, coffee and bakery joint has its own rooftop farm growing ingredients for its dishes, drinks and pastries. Pick up a loaf of the handcrafted organic and seasonal sourdough to scoff at home.

Unit 3d Stamford Works, Gillett Street, Dalston, N16 8JH

brunswickeast.london | ⓘ brunswick_east

8 Lodestar Coffee

This multi-roaster coffee shop keeps Clapton's caffeine levels topped up by providing ever-changing options on espresso, batch and hand brew. The fun occasionally extends into a nighttime cafe offering.

163 Clarence Road, Lower Clapton, E5 8EE

ⓘ lodestarcoffee

9 e5 Bakehouse ⠹

After taking a course in sourdough making, owner Ben reinvented himself as a baker, building a clay oven under a railway arch. These days, that same site is massively expanded and now houses the bakery, a cafe, a store and a coffee roastery. Find a sister site in Poplar.

Arch 395, Mentmore Terrace, Hackney, E8 3PH

e5bakehouse.com | ⓘ e5bakehouse

(10) 215 Hackney Cafe

215 Stoke Newington High Street, Hackney, N16 0LH

215hackney.co.uk | 020 7254 5199

215hackney

Home of baklawa french toast, this Hackney cafe is a hotspot for food influencers who visit – camera app at the ready – to sink their teeth into the famed house specialty. Comprising a fluffy brioche base, pistachio cream, shards of filo pastry and a drizzle of orange and saffron syrup, it's a decadent experience.

What's less documented on the 'gram, however, is 215's first-rate coffee. Dalston's Allpress beans are prepared as a range of silky smooth espresso drinks by skilled baristas and make a mean match to the syrupy toast and other dishes on the Middle Eastern-leaning brunch menu.

🌀 Homemade potato latkes and shakshuka are the savoury house specialities

Influenced by Tel Aviv street food, Lebanese breads, Palestinian comfort food, Syrian platters and Kurdish delicacies, this is fusion cuisine given an East London twist thanks to its use of local produce.

Those watching the pennies will be delighted to learn about the £5 dine-in menu (Monday to Thursday) which includes homemade hummus and boiled eggs with zhoug and fresh pitta, and housemade granola with seasonal fruits.

Established
2019

Key roaster
Allpress Espresso

Brewing method
Espresso

Machine
La Marzocco
Linea Classic

Grinder
Victoria Arduino
Mythos One

Opening hours
Mon-Fri
7am-4pm
Sat-Sun
9am-5pm

(11) The Beehive

305 Cambridge Heath Road, Bethnal Green, E2 9LH

thebeehivelondon.co.uk

🅕 thebeehiveldn 🅞 thebeehiveldn

In the heart of Bethnal Green, you'll find a swarm of busy Bs (B for barista) working away in a space that's all about the three Cs: coffee, creativity and community.

This Beehive is a social enterprise providing delicious refreshment with a side of craft sessions and wellbeing workshops – with the aim of helping local residents thrive.

Powered by a daily batch brew and house espresso roasted by Climpson & Sons, along with a rotating seasonal filter, The Beehive crosses the line between social enterprise and mainstream coffee shop without compromising on quality. The team's vision was *'to create an environment that's warm and accessible to all, not just the usual East London coffee demographic'*. They also provide opportunities for locals to gain experience and integrate (or reintegrate) into society by working at the cafe.

🐝 Everyone's welcome to join the Craft & Company sessions and arty workshops

These friendly volunteers also help make the vibe super welcoming, while customers can do their bit by partaking in the pay-it-forward scheme: paying for a coffee or toast for someone who can't afford it.

Established
2018

Key roaster
Climpson & Sons

Brewing method
Espresso,
batch brew

Machine
La Marzocco
Linea PB 2AV

Grinder
Mahlkonig EK43,
Victoria Arduino
Mythos One

Opening hours
Mon-Fri
8am-5.30pm
Sat
9.30am-5.30pm

12 Paradox Design + Coffee

Find the coffee arm of the Paradox coffee/ design mash-up at Netil Market, surrounded by a curation of food and retail brands. Don't miss the delicious Obadiah house roast.

Netil Market, 13-23 Westgate Street, E8 3RL

welcometotheparadox.com

paradox_design_coffee

13 Ozone Coffee – London Fields

Ozone's London Fields outpost is a great find for on-point food and coffee from New Zealand's pioneering roastery. An indoor canteen with plenty of outdoor seating means you can usually nab a table for breakfast, brunch or lunch.

Emma Street, E2 9AP

ozonecoffee.co.uk | ozonecoffeeuk

14 FORNO

This Italian bakery, pastificio and deli gives visitors the chance to live la dolce vita via traditional Italian delicacies such as veneziana buns and rosemary-spiked focaccia, complemented by silky Allpress Espresso coffee.

322 Andrews Road, E8 4RP

forno.london | forno.london

15 Mae + Harvey

This neighbourhood cafe on Roman Road is a popular local haunt for coffee, breakfast, lunch and weekend brunching. Proper cooking with everything made from scratch is paired with on-point baristery. Lucky locals.

414-416 Roman Road, Bow, E3 5LU

maeandharvey.com | maeandharveycafe

(16) Fink's Chats

62 Chatsworth Road, Homerton, E5 0LS

finks.co.uk

☉ finkschats

This vision in pink is the latest addition to a burgeoning coffee family and joins Fink's Salt & Sweet of Highbury, Fink's Gillespie in Finsbury Park and the brand's other new venture, Fink's Pump House in Clissold Park.

This outpost in Homerton serves everything Fink's is famous for: excellent wines and spirits, Dusty Knuckle bread, next-level sandwiches, the best toasties you're ever likely to scoff (think french onion with comté and gruyère on sourdough), own-baked cakes and, of course, top-notch coffee.

🜂 Feeling the heat? Cool down with a spumone ice cream sandwich and an iced pour

The beans are provided by Scenery Coffee Roasters and served as espresso and filter brews. Pair your pick of the pours with a fondue and kimchi toastie and a slice of buttermilk banana bread. The Fink's team are as good at baking as they are at slinging shots, which is why carbs form the core of the newly expanded food menu. On sunny days, head outdoors to scoff and sip in the new alfresco seating area.

Sustainability is a theme that runs through everything here: the team use planet-positive Wildfarmed flours in their baked goods, and the coffee cups and salad pots are eco-friendly.

Established
2022

Key roaster
Scenery Coffee
Roasters

Brewing method
Espresso, filter

Machine
Victoria Arduino
Eagle One

Grinder
Mazzer Robur

Opening hours
Mon-Fri
8am-4pm
Sat-Sun
9am-4pm

(17) Clarnico Club

1 Tandy Place, Hackney Wick, E20 3AS

sendcoffee.co.uk

clarnicoclub

The biggest of SEND Coffee's speciality cafes in London, Clarnico Club is as interestingly diverse as the community events and training programmes it regularly hosts.

Since the non-profit roastery launched in 2020, it's collaborated with hundreds of young adults with special educational needs and disabilities, helping guide them into careers in the speciality coffee and hospitality industries.

🐾 You know your pup has made it when they land a photo on Clarnico Club's dog wall of fame

Not just a training ground, Clarnico is also a must-visit for a superb coffee-drinking experience. Single-origin SEND beans and a small assortment of ethically-sound guest roasts are fashioned into a range of espresso drinks, batch brews and (season depending) cold brew. You may even be treated to a hand brew if you ask nicely.

Pair your pick of the coffee menu with a freshly made sarnie, pastry or cake, and feed your hunger as you feed your soul by soaking up the good vibes in this light-filled space.

Established
2020

Key roaster
SEND Coffee

Brewing method
Espresso,
batch brew

Machine
La Marzocco KB90

Grinder
Mahlkonig EK43,
Mahlkonig E80,
Victoria Arduino
Mythos One x3

Opening hours
Mon-Fri
7.30am-4pm
Sat-Sun
9am-5pm

(18) Back to Ours

Good Shepherd Studios, 15a Davies Lane, E11 3DR

back-to-ours.com

 back_to_ours_

You have to put in the work to find this emporium of speciality coffee and handcrafted carbs, but the velvety flat whites and lacquered pastries are worth every wrong turn you take to get there.

Sited in the beautiful Victorian building that houses Good Shepherd Studios (a co-working and creative community hub), Back to Ours is only accessible via a hidden entrance at the back of the building. You'll know you're there once you find yourself in a south-facing leafy suntrap perfumed with the intoxicating aroma of just-ground coffee beans.

🌀 Get lost on Wanstead Flats – and discover Leytonstone's best worst-kept secret

Head inside to peruse a menu of espresso drinks and homemade cold brew crafted from Assembly beans, alongside batch filters and pourovers from a rotation of guest roasteries that have included Plot, Curve and Hard Lines. The Back to Ours team are passionate about speciality coffee but wear their knowledge lightly, so don't be intimidated about quizzing them on the beans behind your brew.

Once you've got your liquid libation sorted, pair it with a killer bake – the team source them from The Snapery East – or a delicious brunch dish that's whipped up in-house.

Established
2023

Key roaster
Assembly Coffee

Brewing method
Espresso, batch filter, pourover, cold brew

Machine
La Marzocco
Linea PB ABR

Grinder
Mahlkonig E65S GbW,
Mahlkonig EK43

Opening hours
Mon-Fri
7.30am-4pm
Sat
8am-4pm
Sun
8am-3pm

Nagare Coffee

⑲ **Nagare Coffee**

This beautiful little Japanese-style coffee shop is a delightful pit stop for experiencing brews made with exacting care and served with minimalist elegance. Regular events and creative exhibitions take the experience further.

Ground Floor, 40 Brushfield Street, Spitalfields, E1 6AG

nagare.co.uk | ⓘ nagarecoffee

⑳ **Potter & Reid**

This neighbourhood hangout in the heart of Spitalfields is a find for first-class speciality coffee, fleek food and handpicked natural wines served in contemporary surrounds.

20-22 Toynbee Street, Spitalfields, E1 7NE

potterandreid.com | ⓘ potterandreid

㉑ **TRADE** ⅜

Each of the TRADE cafes enjoys a healthy reputation for own-roasted small-batch coffees, welcoming hospitality and push-the-boat-out breakfasts and lunches. Its Spitalfields location is a favourite for its lovely sun terrace.

47 Commercial Street, Spitalfields, E1 6BD

trade-made.com | ⓘ trade_coffee

㉒ **Grove Lane Deli**

Female-owned GLD's USP is 'nice people making nice coffee, sandwiches and cake'. It couldn't be more accurate: visit for wholesome vibes, a fun and friendly team, stuffed-to-capacity sandwiches and banging Assembly flat whites.

4a Grove Lane, Camberwell, SE5 8SY

grovelanedeli.com | ⓘ grovelanedeli

(23) Mouse Tail Coffee

13 Maritime Street, SE16 7FU

mousetail.co | 07810 835347

mousetailcoffee

First, let's get the obvious question out of the way: why Mouse Tail? It's a reference to the way a rich espresso should subtly curve as it pours into the cup.

If that sounds like next-level attention to detail, it makes sense when you discover Mouse Tail Coffee's sister company is respected roastery Mission Coffee Works, and that the crew recently opened a bakery to provide carby goods which are as high quality as the coffee.

This is a tale of success and good fortune, which grew from a humble one-man coffee van to a collection of cafes across the capital – they're now in Borough, Canada Water, Deptford, Farringdon and Whitechapel. Each has its own aesthetic but all share a welcoming vibe.

🐭 Pair your pick with a cinnamon knot from the Mouse Tail Bakery in Deptford

Visit seven days a week for delicious treats and exceptional service from a team who receive extensive coffee training at the roastery and undertake SCA Professional Barista certifications.

Sample their skills by ordering a Bells espresso – Mission's classic blend that's all dark chocolate, caramel and hazelnut – or the Honduran Meladis Reyes with notes of lemongrass, redcurrant and icing sugar.

Established
2013

Key roaster
Mission
Coffee Works

Brewing method
Espresso,
batch brew

Machine
Sanremo Café Racer

Grinder
Mahlkonig E80 GbW

Opening hours
Mon-Fri
7.30am-6pm
Sat-Sun
8am-6pm

(24) 640East

10 Water Street, Canary Wharf, E14 5GX

640east.co.uk

🟦 640east 📷 640east

640East is a welcome indie find among the skyscrapers and big-brand sprawl of Canary Wharf's shopping areas.

Located on Water Street in the new Wood Wharf development, this is an industrial-style cafe and bar with outdoor seating, decent tunes and a lively buzz.

🔵 Pick up home-brewing gear including V60s, KeepCups, filters and beans from 640East's retail curation

The 640East baristas have their customers' caffeine needs covered whether they need a pre- or post-meeting hit, or are just stopping by during a wander through this immaculate, cosmopolitan part of town.

With Assembly beans in the hopper, and an ever-changing roster of guest roasteries such as Scenery and Square Mile popping up, the coffee focus is on quality London roasts. However, the likes of Danish brand La Cabra and Seville's Ineffable Coffee also rep the European scene.

In summer, the 640East crew create an irresistible festival vibe that pairs perfectly with the flowing drinks. Craft beer and cocktails rub shoulders with kombucha and cold brew, making this a lovely find for a chilled afternoon.

Established
2017

Key roaster
Assembly Coffee

Brewing method
Espresso, batch brew, cold brew, Orea V3

Machine
La Marzocco
Linea PB

Grinder
Mazzer Kold S,
Mahlkonig EK43

Opening hours
Mon-Fri
7.30am-5pm
Sat-Sun
9am-5pm

(25) **Ideal Espresso**

Greenwich Market, SE10 9HZ

ideal-espresso.com

🅵 Ideal Espresso Greenwich 🅾 ideal_espresso

It is exceptional attention to detail that makes a great speciality coffee venue stand the test of time, and this stall in Greenwich Market is a perfect example. By striving to craft perfection with each cortado and cappuccino, Ideal has become a speciality stalwart that's thrived for over a decade.

Visitors can track down a handcrafted brew 364 days a year – it's only on Christmas Day that the crew put their feet up and let their loyal customers see to their own caffeination.

Mission Coffee Works provides the beans at this market venue, while a prized VA White Eagle Leva machine extracts the goods. And ditch any ill-advised notion of a coffee stall delivering anything less than the kind of perfect pour or beautifully executed coffee you'd find in a slicker setting – as Ideal's Instagram grid can attest.

☕ Hot day? Enjoy the tingly thrills of Ideal's iced coffee

The small team have been delivering the goods for years and know how to serve up a first-rate hospitality experience, with as much emphasis placed on having a natter with the customers as on speedy service.

Established
2013

Key roaster
Mission Coffee Works

Brewing method
Espresso

Machine
Victoria Arduino White Eagle Leva

Grinder
Mahlkonig E65S GbW

Opening hours
Mon
9am–5pm
Tue–Sun
8am–5pm

26 Söderberg – East Dulwich ✌

This baby of the Söderberg family (comprising seven sites in Edinburgh and one on Berwick Street) arrived in 2023. Newbies can expect the Swedish cafe-bakery to deliver an authentic fika fix of Scandi-style dishes and quality coffee.

36 Lordship Lane, East Dulwich, SE22 8HJ

soderberg.uk | 🅞 soderbergbakery

27 Nola Coffee

Peckham's effortlessly pared-back coffee spot deals in single-origin, sustainably sourced beans, which are available to buy in-store. There are also ethical teas, juices and hot chocolate to slurp, plus locally baked sourdough toasties, bagels and pastries to scoff.

224 Rye Lane, Peckham, SE15 4NL

nolacoffee.co.uk | 🅞 drinkatnola

28 Good as Gold ✌

Combining experience in illustration, fine dining and antipodean coffee culture, founders Anthony and Tom brought a golden coffee experience to Brockley – and more recently to a new location in Hackney. Dinner is served on Thursday and Friday nights.

209 Mantle Road, Brockley, SE4 2EW

goodasgoldldn.com | 🅞 goodasgoldldn

29 Oscar's SE13

This friendly neighbourhood coffee shop serves speciality brews alongside fresh food and bakes. Take your order to the hidden suntrap garden out the back to sip and munch in verdant loveliness.

48 Ladywell Road, SE13 7UZ

cafeoscars.co.uk | 🅞 cafe_oscars

A WAY FOR ALL

Independent since 1970.

For over fifty years, we have crafted our own way of working in coffee. Still a third-generation family-owned green coffee merchant today, we continue on this path, prioritising long-term sustainable relationships.

Our approach is to match the right coffee with the right people, along the whole supply chain. So whatever quality coffee means to you, you'll feel right at home with us.

(30) Servesmiths

From the satiny Assembly-bean coffees to the bundles of fresh local bakes, Servesmiths' objective is for each sip and bite to reflect south London's creative and artisanal community.

3a Doggett Road, Catford, SE6 4PZ

servesmiths.com | ⊙ servesmiths

(31) Four Boroughs ⅍

Four Boroughs serves Assembly coffee, plus finds from guest roasteries, at its outposts at Crystal Palace, Loughborough Junction and South Norwood. Check out its Shopify page for funky merch to rep your new fave coffee shop.

10 Church Road, Crystal Palace, SE19 2ET

⊙ four_boroughs

SOUTH

South London cafes

Putney

Wimbledon

Morden

Locations are approximate

Battersea

10

11

14

Stockwell

13

12

4

16

Brixton

Clapham

Herne Hill

9

15

17

Find more
cafes in this area on
the East London
map on page 68

8

Balham

Tooting Broadway

Streatham

5

7

19

Beckenham

Croydon

18

South Croydon

20

140 Upper Richmond Road, Putney, SW15 2SW

moniescoffee.com

🇫 moniescoffeebar 🇴 moniescoffeebar

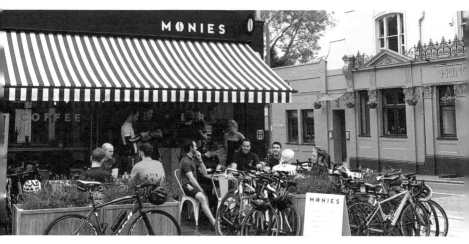

With the aim of bringing a scoop of the good vibes from his home county of Cornwall to East Putney, Rob Monies has created a speciality coffee bar with cocktails which also operates as a brunch spot, deli and bottle shop. The result is sunny community vibes – whatever the weather.

🔵 Mix it up with an Espresso Martini milkshake or glass of English wine

Locals love Rob's coffee but also drop in for the homemade cinnamon buns, banana bread, cheese-stuffed croissants and artisan sarnies (the chicken caesar toastie is a fan favourite). Pretty much everything is made from scratch on-site by the kitchen team and resident baker each morning. Swing by early doors to sample the freshly baked granola or luscious overnight oats served with a knockout cup of coffee.

Coffee mostly comes from the other end of the UK, roasted in Fife by Modern Standard, although Wales' Hard Lines, Shoreditch's Ozone and Cornwall's Yallah Coffee also guest.

Don't leave without having a snoop at the shelves showcasing Cornish produce, including the likes of wild garlic pesto and natural English wine.

Established
2021

Key roaster
Modern Standard Coffee

Brewing method
Espresso, batch brew, V60

Machine
Victoria Arduino Black Eagle

Grinder
Mahlkonig E65S GbW, Victoria Arduino Mythos Two

Opening hours
Mon-Fri
7.30am-4pm
Sat
8am-4pm
Sun
8.30am-4pm

(2) Another Brother

Sheffield-born bros Joey and Eddy create coffee shops with community vibes. Indie roastery Curious Roo heads the line-up of quality suppliers that have joined the family. Find more brotherly love at sister sites in Shepherd's Bush and Hammersmith.

187 Putney Bridge Road, SW15 2NZ

anotherbrother.co | (O) anotherbrotherldn

(3) Milk No Milk

Clean lines and minimalism are the backdrop for a warm welcome and beautifully brewed speciality pours at this neighbourhood coffee shop. An extensive breakfast menu complements the caffeinated offering.

281 Kingston Road, Wimbledon, SW20 8LB

milknomilk.co.uk

(4) Story Coffee

On the corner of St John's Hill is where it all began for Story Coffee. Swing by its OG coffee shop site for a brew to-go and watch from the window hatch as the pro baristas work their magic on speciality beans.

115 St John's Hill, SW11 1SZ

storycoffee.co.uk | (O) storycoffeeldn

(5) Juliets Quality Foods

Food is crafted with as much care as the coffee at this funky neighbourhood cafe. House specials include the freddo cappuccino: single-origin espresso over ice, with tonka bean caramel and cold whipped-milk foam.

110 Mitcham Road, Tooting Broadway, SW17 9NG

juliets.london | (O) julietsqualityfood

⑥ Metronome Coffee House

8 Crown Lane, Morden, SM4 5BL

metronome.life | 020 8540 6107

f metronomelife ⊙ metronomelife

© Tony Murray

Background music is an integral part of the coffee shop experience, but there aren't many places that appreciate the relationship between sips and sounds like Morden's cafe/recording-studio mash-up.

On-point playlists are guaranteed at this dynamic space, which is as renowned for its live-music events as for its stellar coffee line-up. A state-of-the-art Genelec sound system delivers the music with sparkling clarity that's matched only by the whistle-clean filter coffees made from Chimney Fire Coffee beans.

🔵 Cup holders look familiar? They're made out of oat milk cartons

Espresso, batch filters, cold brew and pourovers are diligently created by a talented band of baristas, and it's always worth asking which guest coffees are headlining that day. For sustenance to pair with your caffeine pick, check out the curation of fresh pastries.

The crew also run an events calendar which features an eclectic range of live music – from piano recitals to the returning pub orchestra – alongside community workshops and art exhibitions. On Wednesday to Saturday evenings, Metronome morphs into a wine bar specialising in low-intervention wines and Espresso Martinis.

Established
2020

Key roaster
Chimney Fire Coffee

Brewing method
V60, batch filter

Machine
Conti

Grinder
Compaq

Opening hours
Mon-Tue
6.30am-4pm
Wed-Fri
6.30am-10pm
Sat
8.30am-10pm
Sun
8.30am-4pm

⑦ Cut the Mustard ☕

This Tooting bakery pairs quality carbs with top-notch coffees to-go. Don't leave without picking up a loaf of country sourdough 'Frank' – named after owner Jimmy's grandfather. Find a second outlet on nearby Franciscan Road.

68 Moyser Road, Furzedown, Tooting, SW16 6SQ

cutthemustardcafe.com | ⓘ cutthemustardcafe

⑧ The Apple Blue ☕

Swan-adorned flat whites, peach-cobbler cheesecake and pecan crumble croissants are just three examples of the deliciousness going down at this Balham cafe. The Volcano-roasted brews are also a wicked match to the savoury dishes.

212 Balham High Road, SW12 9BS

theappleblue.com | ⓘ theapplebluebalham

⑨ SHED Clapham ☕

This coffee and wine shop is part of a series of co-working studios for movers and shakers in the city's creative industries. Drop by (no laptop required) to imbibe the arty buzz and superior speciality brews.

Clapham South Station, Clapham, SW12 9DU

shedlondon.com | ⓘ shedlondonshops

⑩ Nostos Coffee – Battersea ☕

Discover a meticulous coffee experience at the original Nostos coffee shop, open all week for own-roasted beans, multiple serve styles and exceptional service. Visit the St James's outlet to try a freeze-distilled flat white.

10a Battersea Park Road, Battersea, SW8 4FF

nostoscoffee.co.uk | ⓘ nostoscoffee

(11) Moonstruck Cafe

153 South Lambeth Road, SW8 1XN

moonstruck.cafe | 020 3900 2413

moonstruck.cafe

To be moonstruck means to be madly in love with something – an apt name for a cafe so utterly devoted to speciality coffee.

Intrepid caffeine fans hunt out this SW8 spot in search of their perfect match, whether that's in the form of a dalliance with the fruit-forward house espresso or a fling with a brew from the frozen coffee menu (over 60 options and counting). PLOT Roasting supplies the bulk of the beans for the house serves, but is accompanied by an array of guest roasts from international roasteries which are switched up with every new moon.

🌀 Check out indie art gallery, Under The Spell, located in the basement

If you're not yet ready to commit to a specific bean and brew-method combo, let the knowledgeable baristas craft you a guest-coffee flight featuring the same guest beans served three ways: pourover, single espresso and mini flat white.

There are some lovely spots in the cafe's calming surrounds in which to savour your sip. The interiors were designed by London's YAM Studios, drawing on Scandi, Japanese and Belgian influences. Minimalist detailing with clean lines, warm colours and tactile textures create a relaxing hangout where coffee love can blossom.

Established
2024

Key roaster
PLOT Roasting

Brewing method
Espresso,
batch brew,
pourover

Machine
La Marzocco
Linea PB Custom

Grinder
Weber Workshops
EG-1, Mahlkonig
E65S GbW,
Mahlkonig EK43

Opening hours
Mon-Sun
8am-4pm

(12) Door – Coffee Bar

244 Ferndale Road, Brixton, SW9 8FR

doorcoffeebar.com | 020 3876 0876

doorcoffeebarlondon

The Door is open! This new coffee bar is the first collaborative shopfront for successful sister brands Assembly Coffee and Volcano Coffee Works. Both speciality roasteries share a commitment to quality while sourcing coffees for two different types of customer: entry-level sippers and seasoned enthusiasts. As a result, Door is a welcoming environment where visitors can take their first steps into speciality coffee or taste some of the world's rarest beans from the most progressive producers.

🌀 Seasonal serves include the likes of a coffee-infused non-alc spritz

There are always three espresso coffees available behind the bar: Volcano's Mount Blend for milk–based drinks, Assembly's House Espresso (best taken black), and a third rotating Assembly roast that delivers a flavour-packed punch served either way. A daily batch-filter coffee menu is also available, while pourover fans should ask for the off-menu dealer's choice to source a sip that's rather special.

The 'Open Doors' open day each season provides an excellent portal into the world of coffee tasting. Baristas brew samples of coffees from across its roasteries' catalogues, host latte-art masterclasses and give attendees the chance to geek out over speciality coffee.

Established
2023

Key roaster
Assembly Coffee,
Volcano Coffee Works

Brewing method
Espresso,
batch filter,
pourover

Machine
Victoria Arduino Eagle
One 2AV

Grinder
Sanremo X-One,
Victoria Arduino
Mythos One

Opening hours
Mon-Fri
7am-3pm
Sat
9am-4pm

13 Bobo & Wild ✂

Cafes by Shoreditch Park, Clapham Common and South Woodford deal in all-day coffee and brunch. Enjoy a caffeine fix from own-roasted beans, then stick around for dishes like wild mushrooms, truffle eggs and parmesan snow on rosemary focaccia.

18 Clapham Common South Side, SW4 7AB

boboandwild.co.uk | ⊙ boboandwild

14 Common Cafe Shop Wine

This eco cafe, store and bar in a former chemist's deals in all things local and organic. Swing by for everything from Assembly coffee to sustainable homewares. Visit on Fridays and Saturdays for late-night cocktails in the vintage apothecary bar.

17 The Pavement, Clapham, SW4 0HY

commonclapham.com | ⊙ commonclapham

15 Stir Coffee Brixton

Caffeine fiends go stir-crazy for this coffee shop in Brixton with its cracking bill of global guest roasts, delicious bites and laid-back vibe. Sit in to feast on fresh edibles and pick up an array of international beans to-go.

111 Brixton Hill, Brixton, SW2 1AA

stircoffee.co.uk | ⊙ stir_coffee

Common Cafe Shop Wine

(16) The Common Espresso Bar

10 Clapham Park Road, Clapham, SW4 7BB

thecommonespressobar.co.uk | 020 3490 0431

 thecommonespressobar thecommonespressobar

Brewing up connections in the community through speciality coffee and delicious food, this authentic coffee shop around the corner from Clapham Common Station teems with locals enjoying their daily caffeine hit and visitors who are excited to have stumbled upon somewhere specialising in the good stuff.

Community vibes are evident from the moment you step inside: regulars are known by name and their coffee orders memorised, pups are treated like royalty with special treats, eco-conscious customers like the recyclable cups and biodegradable straws, and the friendly team and photo-adorned walls create a homely atmosphere.

⚙ Homemade treats include vegetarian, vegan and gluten-free options

The crew are loyal to Union Hand-Roasted beans, and its house blend Bright Note (sourced from Colombia and Brazil) is used to craft bright and uplifting brews yielding notes of tangerine, chocolate and macadamia. Out-of-the-ordinary latte art takes the coffee experience a step further. Those seeking less caffeinated refreshment are well catered for with freshly squeezed juices, smoothies, chai lattes and hot chocolate.

Perch at a window seat and enjoy a spot of people watching as you pair your brew with a cheesy toastie, pastry or cake. In a rush? Explore the excellent grab-and-go options.

Established
2017

Key roaster
Union Hand-Roasted Coffee

Brewing method
Espresso, AeroPress

Machine
La Marzocco Linea Classic

Grinder
Sanremo SR70

Opening hours
Mon-Fri
7.30am-4pm
Sat
8.30am-4pm
Sun
9.30am-4pm

(17) **Perks & White**

Ticket Hall - Herne Hill Station, Railton Road, Herne Hill, SE24 0JW

perksandwhite.com

perksandwhite

With outposts at Herne Hill and Tulse Hill stations, as well as a new venue at Loughborough Junction station, this decade-long favourite is moving down the line.

The focus is on sustainability and lasting relationships at Perks & White – including with its customers, staff, the local community, suppliers and business partners. The glorious house espresso, made in partnership with Volcano in Brixton, encapsulates this approach. These house beans originate from the Santo de Minas region of Brazil and reveal distinctive notes of dark chocolate, toffee, and plum.

🌱 Forgot your reusable? The takeaway cups are 100% compostable and recyclable

Through Volcano, the cafe is part of the Sombra Agroforestry Project, which aims to promote sustainable coffee farming using shade-grown systems and organic methods, without the use of artificial fertilisers. The benefits of this approach include shielding the land from the extreme weather conditions exacerbated by climate change in Brazil, enhancing drainage and safeguarding the life of the soil.

Experience the good vibes for yourself in brews complemented by light breakfasts, lunchtime snacks and cakes from local artisans Maya's Cookhouse, Food By Toby and BreadBread. And don't leave without beans to-go from roasters such as Stay High, Dark Arts and Cuppers Choice.

Established
2014

Key roaster
Volcano Coffee Works,
Assembly Coffee,
Stay High

Brewing method
Espresso, batch filter,
cold brew

Machine
La Marzocco, Linea PB,
Victoria Arduino
Eagle One

Grinder
Mahlkonig E80,
Mahlkonig EK43,
Victoria Arduino
Mythos One

Opening hours
Mon-Fri
7.30am-3pm
Sat
8.30am-3.30pm
Sun
9am-4pm

(18) Crushed Bean

81 High Street, Croydon, CR0 1QE

crushedbeancroydon.com

crushedbeancroydon

Radiating positive vibes, this proudly LGBT-owned-and-run cafe offers an inclusive and welcoming environment for Croydon's coffee aficionados.

Following a recent refurbishment, Crushed Bean has a sleek minimalist interior built around a brew bar lined with coffee gear and freshly made bakes. Sunlight pours into the space (which explains the vitality of its houseplants) and its window bench is the prime spot to enjoy your morning brew with a hit of vit D. There's also a cosy seating area in the basement for those seeking a quiet vibe.

Calm any caffeine jitters with a citrusy mint magic tea

The clued-up baristas craft most of the coffee menu using beans from Bristol's Clifton Coffee Roasters, but guest roasteries Outpost, Monmouth and Square Mile also feature occasionally.

Brews are complemented by sourdough sarnies and creative homemade cakes (the light and fluffy Japanese cheesecake is a must). Keen to try something new? Off-piste pairings include an earl-grey rose latte with a Mumbai cheese toastie.

Established
2017

Key roaster
Clifton Coffee
Roasters

Brewing method
Espresso,
V60, filter

Machine
La Marzocco
Linea PB

Grinder
Victoria Arduino
Mythos One

Opening hours
Mon-Fri
7.30am-3pm
Sat
9am-3pm

trewithen

DELICIOUSLY CORNISH DAIRY

CREAMY CORNISH
BARISTA MILK

HIGH IN PROTEIN AND
EXTRA CREAMY

DESIGNED BY
BARISTA'S
FOR BARISTA'S

THE SECRET
INGREDIENT FOR THE
PERFECT LATTE
AT HOME!

SEE FOR YOURSELF

FROTHS LIKE A DREAM
FOR THAT SMOOTH,
DELICIOUS FINISH

 trewithendairy.co.uk   trewithen_dairy   TrewithenDairy

⑲ Shotsmiths

With its bold turquoise-blue frontage and perma-busy flow of coffee sippers, passersby can't help themselves from dropping into Shotsmiths. Those who step inside discover an emporium of top-drawer coffee and swoonsome carbs.

73 Beckenham Road, Beckenham, BR3 4PR

shotsmiths.com | ⓘ shotsmiths

⑳ FILTR by Coromandel Coast ୪ᐤ

FILTR sources and roasts sustainable shade-grown coffee from southern India, which reveals exotic notes from the tropical fruit trees it grows under. Taste the range at this coffee and zero-waste lifestyle store.

53 Limpsfield Road, South Croydon, CR2 9LB

coromandelcoast.co.uk | ⓘ filtr_coffee

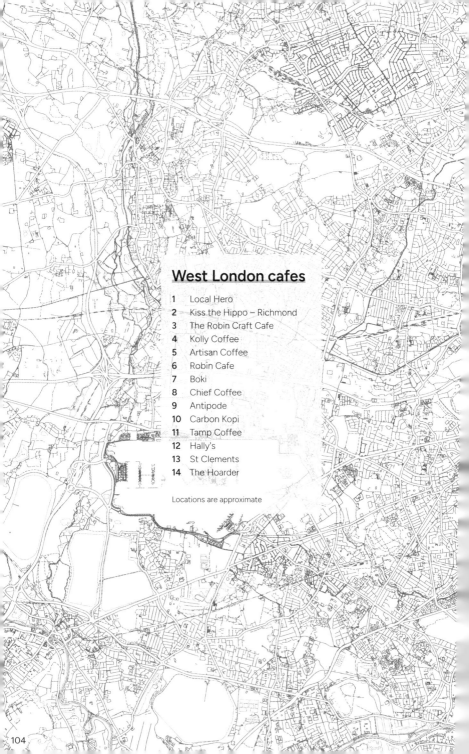

West London cafes

Locations are approximate

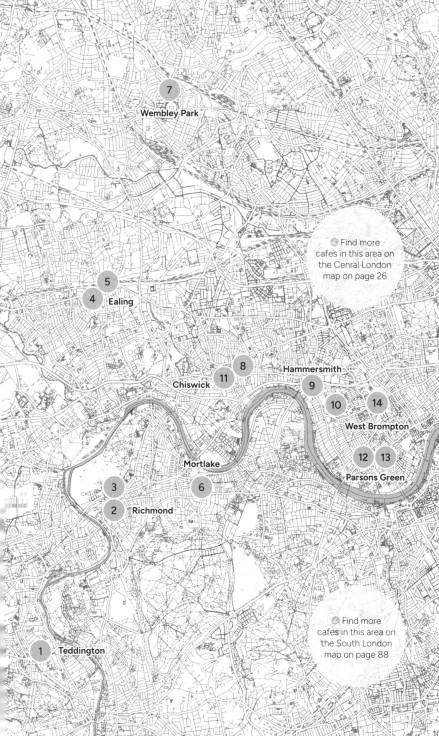

Find more cafes in this area on the Cenral London map on page 26

Find more cafes in this area on the South London map on page 88

7 Wembley Park

5
4 Ealing

8
11 Chiswick

Hammersmith
9

10

14

West Brompton

12 13

Parsons Green

Mortlake

6

3

2 Richmond

1 Teddington

① Local Hero

59 High Street, Teddington, TW11 8HA

localherocoffee.co.uk

🔲 localhero.coffee

Hundreds of hours of research, testing and cupping went into producing and perfecting Local Hero's own-roasted signature house blend, Soul Man. Happily, each of those hours and every experimental batch was worth it for the rich and silky espresso it yields.

Soul Man was crafted to complement milk-based coffees and creates a knockout flat white. However, those who prefer their brews served black are also catered for thanks to a fruit-forward single origin that's also roasted in-house.

☕ The house spesh – espresso ristretto – is all syrupy caramel sweetness

The meticulous care that's poured into roasting these coffees is mirrored in the team's cheerful service and commitment to making the cafe a community hangout where baristas know each regular by name and their brew preference by heart.

Equally as delectable is the satiation found via the menu of focaccia toasties, brioche breakfast burgers and brunch classics. More delicious fare can also be discovered at Local Hero outposts in Fulham and Kingston. Courgette carrot fritters are the house speciality and tend to sell out fast at all three sites. Served with avocado, aubergine relish, toasted seeds and carrot puree, they can be pimped with optional extras including poached eggs, halloumi and smoked streaky bacon.

Established
2004

Key roaster
Local Hero

Brewing method
Espresso,
cold brew

Machine
Victoria Arduino
Black Eagle
Maverick

Grinder
Mahlkonig E65S

Opening hours
Mon-Fri
7.30am-4pm
Sat-Sun
8am-4pm

② Kiss the Hippo – Richmond ౿

The innovative and sustainable speciality roastery has cafes in key locations across London, including this one (the original) in Richmond. Own-roasted beans are showcased in espresso drinks and pourovers on the brew bar.

21 Sheen Road, Richmond, TW9 1AD

kissthehippo.com | 🅞 kissthehippo

③ The Robin Craft Cafe ౿

The quality coffee at this Thai-owned cafe is as delightful as the quirky hand-crafted cups in which it is served. Cakes and bakes make good bedfellows for the caffeination, but the homemade Thai food is too good to miss.

55 Kew Road, Richmond, TW9 2NQ

🅞 therobincraftcafe

④ Kolly Coffee

This speciality find within the Spaces office building keeps workers' caffeine levels expertly topped up via its banging brews. The speciality sips are not just for the Spaces crew, however, as Kolly is open to the public too.

71-75 Uxbridge Road, Ealing, W5 5SL

kollycoffee.com | 🅞 kollycoffee

⑤ Artisan Coffee ౿

Artisan Coffee's Ealing outpost deals in flawless coffees – crafted using Curious Roo speciality beans – served in a home-from-home environment. Want to brush up on your brewing skills? Coffee training courses are available.

32 New Broadway, Ealing, W5 2XA

artisancoffee.co.uk | 🅞 artisan_coffee

⑥ Robin Cafe

38 Sheen Lane, SW14 8LW

craftbytherobin.co.uk

🅵 therobincraftcafe 🅾 therobincraftcafe

More than just a spot for a quick caffeine fix, this charming Sheen Lane cafe delivers a feelgood hit of ASMR in every visit. The tactile joy of sipping coffee from Robin Cafe's own hand-thrown pottery is combined with the background whoosh of the steam wand and the fragrant aroma of Asian-inspired dishes wafting from the kitchen, delivering a feast for the senses.

Add a touch of theatre by opting for an Origami pourover and watch as the barista precision-brews Square Mile coffee via the Japanese fluted dripper. Vietnamese-style coffee is another signature serve, in which a deeper roast is brewed using a phin filter and combined with condensed milk. The guest roasts are also worth exploring and supplied by roasteries such as Kiss the Hippo and Vietnamese Coffee Co.

🐦 Check out the range of house-made ceramics available to buy

Pair your drinks with delicious bites such as homemade Japanese buns and honey toast, or more substantial eats like Thai red curry. And keep an eye on socials for news of pop-up feast nights (and extended opening hours) in the summertime.

Established
2014

Key roaster
Square Mile
Coffee Roasters

Brewing method
Espresso, pourover,
batch filter, drip

Machine
Victoria Arduino
Black Eagle

Grinder
Victoria Arduino
Mythos One,
Mahlkonig EK43

Opening hours
Mon-Fri
8am–4pm
Sat-Sun
9am–4pm
(seasonal opening hours)

Chief Coffee

⑦ Boki 🎱

Part of the BOXPARK Wembley massive, this kiosk from Boki (find its brother cafe in Aldgate) is a popular pit-stop for those wanting to sink a proper coffee before hitting Wembley Stadium.

Unit 2, BOXPARK, Wembley Park, Wembley, HA9 0JT

bokicoffee.com | 📷 bokicoffee

⑧ Chief Coffee

One third speciality coffee shop, one third Japanese arcade and one third pinball lounge, this eclectic venue combines play with speciality coffee to awesome effect.

Turnham Green Terrace Mews, W4 1QU

📷 chief_coffee

⑨ Antipode

A slice of sunny Melbourne awaits at this easygoing cafe and bar in Hammersmith. Visit for smooth speciality coffee, low-intervention wines, Aussie craft beers and a gnarly brunch.

28 Fulham Palace Road, Hammersmith, W6 9PH

📷 antipodelondon

⑩ Carbon Kopi 🎱

Each cup of coffee at this Hammersmith fave replicates the last in quality and consistency. The bean offering is switched up regularly and delicious guest roasts are usually available.

Baron's Court Store, 11 Margravine Road, Hammersmith, W6 8LS

carbonkopi.com | 📷 carbonkopi

1 Devonshire Road, W4 2EU

tampcoffee.co.uk

 tampcoffeelondon tampcoffee

© Natalia Ruszczyk

For cracking coffee with a rustic aesthetic (and sharp merch), trot over to Tamp in Chiswick.

Only high-scoring speciality beans make the grade at this friendly neighbourhood cafe – usually a washed single origin in the espresso hopper, plus some quirky natural or fermented beans on filter. Since 2023, the team have sourced, imported and roasted all their own beans, allowing them to step up the quality and traceability. A shining example is Tamp's Filter Colombia from producer Nestro Lasso of El Diviso farm. A sidra varietal with a score of 89, it goes through a natural anaerobic process before reaching Tamp's roaster, where notes of bubblegum, strawberry candy and chocolate truffle are brought to the fore.

⏱ Loved your brew? Stock up on beans to-go from Tamp's range of own-roasted coffees

'We only source the best of the best, in everything – from coffee beans and milk to pastry and the ingredients for our bakery produce,' says director Dorian Needs, who keeps Tamp resolutely independent.

With no plans to open more sites, there is constant reinvestment in the cafe and its offering. Take a seat out front and soak up the assured, relaxed vibe.

Established
2014

Key roaster
Tamp Coffee

Brewing method
Espresso, pourover

Machine
La Marzocco KB90

Grinder
Mahlkonig
E65S GbW × 2,
Mahlkonig EK43

Opening hours
Mon-Fri
7.30am-3.30pm
Sat-Sun
8am-4pm

Hally's

12 Hally's

California meets Parsons Green at this cafe that's all white wood panelling and bifold doors to let the light in. Dark Arts brews are supported by smoothies, fresh food and boutique wines. Take the Cali vibes next level at the weekend with a bottomless brunch.

60 New Kings Road, Parsons Green, SW6 4LS

hallyslondon.com | 📷 hallyslondon

13 St Clements

Good brunch begins with great coffee and a belter of a brew awaits at this cafe, which is dedicated to the late-morning ritual. Bag a cosy window seat or a spot on the sunny terrace to appreciate seasonal brunch dishes and single-origin sips.

201 New Kings Road, Parsons Green, SW6 4SR

stclementscafe.co.uk | 📷 stclementscafe

14 The Hoarder

Tracking down this neighbourhood coffee shop on Lillie Road is easy thanks to its bright green exterior and bold signage. The tough part is deciding which flavour-popping roast to pick and what to bag from the retail shelves packed with artisan snacks and craft bottles.

16 Lillie Road, SW6 1TS

📷 thehoarder

Discover some
of the artisan
roasteries keeping
London's indie cafes
topped up with speciality
beans, and discover new
favourites to fill your
own home hopper

London roasteries

Locations are approximate

West Kilburn

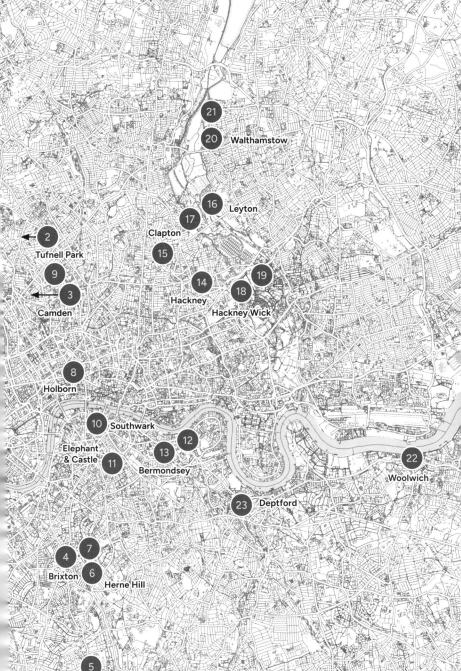

2
Tufnell Park

9
3
Camden

8
Holborn

21
20 Walthamstow

16 Leyton
17
Clapton
15

14
Hackney
18 19
Hackney Wick

10 Southwark
12
Elephant 13
& Castle 11
Bermondsey

23 Deptford

22
Woolwich

4 7
Brixton 6
Herne Hill

5
Norwood

1 Coborn Coffee

The Goods Yard, Station Terrace, NW10 5RS

coborncoffee.com

 coborn.coffee

Coborn is a newbie roastery on London's speciality scene, and one with female empowerment and fairness at its heart.

One of the ways the microroastery's team are living the values behind Coborn's *'fresh, fair, fun'* mantra is by only buying beans from majority women-owned farms, microlots and cooperatives.

Founders Justin and Kenny (pictured) reference the coffee-growing industry being slanted in favour of men, saying: *'The women at the farms are powerhouses and deserve the plaudits, pay and recognition their male counterparts receive.'*

The team recently established a direct-trade relationship with Juliana Guevara, a farm owner in Huila, Colombia. The partnership formed after Zoom conversations in which the pair learnt that Juliana wanted to switch from using bean importers to ensure her greens were sent as fresh as possible to roasters – a wish the pair are fulfilling.

'The RHOC acronym references the Real Housewives of Clapton Instagram account'

Coborn's collection of beans includes RHOC from Las Hortensias, a third-generation coffee farm run by the Albir sisters in Nicaragua. The coffee features notes of orange wine and pineapple and is named after women living a little closer to home: the acronym references the Real Housewives of Clapton Instagram account which is vocal in its appreciation of orange wine.

Established
2023

Roaster make & size
Genio Pro 8kg

Conscious

Tufnell Park, Islington, N19 5LD

consciousspeciality.com | 07590 310156

 consciousspeciality consciousspeciality

To be conscious is to be aware, self-reflective and make considered choices, which is exactly how founders Lea and Culainn approach working within the speciality coffee sphere.

Specialising in small-batch, high-quality single origins from Peru, Bolivia and Colombia, the duo seek out and work with individual producers and community projects. They are dedicated to supporting small-scale farming, sustainable agricultural practices and the production of excellent coffee. 'Our coffees are sweet, clean and vibrant,' says Lea. 'Every single estate coffee is named after the producer – from Raul Flores' caturra (a juicy cup that tastes like tropical fruit punch) to Jenry Perez's geisha with its notes of white peach and honey.'

'Our coffees are sweet, clean and vibrant'

By continually refining their roasting process, Culainn and Lea ensure that each coffee clearly expresses its cultivar and process, highlighting the talent and work that goes into its production. The team's talents have been validated externally too: Culainn is an award winner, securing Best Espresso Experience, Best Filter Experience and Overall Champion at Extracted Development's inaugural competition in 2023.

Home brewers can get in on the act by taking out a Conscious Choice subscription: 'Think of it like your local barista getting to know you, but online,' says Lea.

Established
2022

Roaster make & size
Giesen W15A 15kg

3 SEND Coffee

47-49 Camden Road, NW1 9SL

sendcoffee.co.uk

☐ sendcoffee

Since its inception in 2020, non-profit coffee roastery and training organisation SEND has seen hundreds of young adults with special educational needs and disabilities become SCA-qualified baristas and lead fulfilling roles within the inclusive speciality coffee industry.

Through its comprehensive one-year barista course, learners develop independence, confidence and barista skills, with training drawing upon SCA certification, competition score sheets and insights from seasoned baristas across the UK.

Immersive courses take place at SEND Coffee's cafe-training spaces across the city (Curators Coffee on Cullum Street, Hidden Coffee in Camden and Clarinco Club in Hackney Wick), with students working closely alongside mentors in cafe environments to crack the art of coffee brewing and cultivate essential hospitality skills.

'Learners develop independence, confidence and barista skills'

Although the primary objective is to empower people facing adversity and help them into coffee careers – which has won SEND numerous awards – producing exceptional coffee is still of paramount importance to the team.

Try the roastery's single-origin beans via its online shop (all proceeds go directly to its mentorship programmes). Or visit one of the cafes where precision-trained baristas and Q-grader-approved coffees deliver a cracking caffeinated experience.

Established
2020

Roaster make & size
Giesen 25kg

④ Assembly Coffee

244 Ferndale Road, Brixton, SW9 8FR

assemblycoffee.co.uk | 020 3105 1787

f assemblyroast ⓞ assemblyroast

In 2014, a small group of people working for Volcano Coffee Works brought together the UK's leading independent coffee shops and restaurants to create a blueprint for best practice. After six months, they had a clear vision: to source and roast coffees for the end consumer, to adapt depending on the data, to always challenge perceptions of value and to operate sustainably. At Assembly, the whole is greater than the sum of its parts and everything can always be better.

'Assembly (and Volcano) became the first roastery in the country to hold B Corp and carbon-neutral certification'

Not only are the coffees the pinnacle of quality, but they're also created with fairness in mind. Assembly supports farming communities with whom it has in-person relationships. For instance, in Fazenda Mio in Brazil, Assembly is funding a project to reforest 60,000 trees and coffee plants to help create a biodiverse environment with shade, soil moisture and air humidity. The goal is to prove that native wildlife can thrive alongside farming activities, helping protect the future of Brazilian coffee for all.

In 2022, Assembly (and Volcano) became the first roastery in the country to hold B Corp and carbon-neutral certification. Visit Door, the coffee bar at this Brixton HQ, to experience Assembly up close.

Established
2015

Roaster make & size
Loring S35,
Kestrel 35kg,
Loring S70
Kestrel 70kg

DRWakefield
EST. 1970

COFFEE FOR ALL

Doing the right thing.

It's a sentiment that guides everything we do, from our relationships to our coffees and projects. Since 1970, doing what's right has been at our heart.

Our mission is to connect coffee producers with coffee roasters. By collaborating with other independent businesses, we strive to be a catalyst for sustainable coffee for generations to come.

www.drwakefield.com

5 Volcano Coffee Works

1 Beadman Street, West Croydon, SE27 0DN

volcanocoffeeworks.com | 020 3876 0876

volcanocoffeeworks volcanocoffeeworks

If there's a way to make speciality coffee better for the planet, coffee growers, brewers or drinkers, Volcano Coffee Works is on it. Led by founder Kurt Stewart (pictured), Volcano buys the best beans – not the cheapest ones – and pays farmers above typical Fairtrade wages. The beans are then roasted in small batches.

Volcano was a pioneer in putting speciality coffee into pods and one of the first coffee companies to become a B Corp. As the team mantra goes: *'Great coffee can change more than just your morning; it can change the world.'*

Kurt and team source beans from Brazil, El Salvador, Colombia, Ethiopia, India and Peru in the creation of cracking roasts such as Sombra, a Brazilian coffee with notes of toffee when served with milk, as well as dark chocolate, hazelnut and plum. It's a collab coffee with Brazil's Fazenda Mio and the Instituto do Espirito Santo – the product of an agroforestry and coffee-farming-system project that aims to eliminate mono-crop culture in Brazilian coffee farming.

'Great coffee can change more than just your morning; it can change the world'

Volcano's Brixton Blend is worth a special mention too. The roastery's first combination of coffee species conilon and arabica, it showcases nuttiness, soft acidity and notes of cacao, orange rind and liquorice.

Established
2010

Roaster make & size
Loring S70
Peregrine 70kg,
Loring S35
Kestrel 35kg,
Loring S15 Falcon 15kg

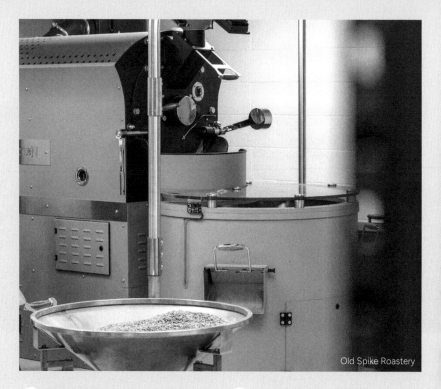
Old Spike Roastery

6 Press Coffee & Co

At Press, high volumes of coffee are bronzed using high-tech equipment and sustainable practices. Cropster roasting technology gives the family-run team (one of whom is an arabica Q grader) the ability to replicate roast profiles and guarantee consistent quality, roast after roast.

Unit 16, Bessemer Park, 250
Milkwood Road, SE24 0HG

presscoffee.london | ⊙ presscoffeelondon

7 Old Spike Roastery

This social enterprise has been at the forefront of using coffee as a vehicle for social change. Old Spike primarily helps to reduce homelessness through training and employment in speciality coffee, via its state-of-the-art barista training academy.

Unit 1, LJ Works, 7 Gastineau Yard, SW9 7FA

oldspikeroastery.com | ⊙ oldspikeroast

8 Catalyst

This small-batch roastery deals exclusively in blends, eschewing single origins and mixing things up to achieve one-of-a-kind coffees. Catalyst prides itself on sourcing ethically, supporting two different farmers with each offering.

48 Grays Inn Road, Chancery Lane, WC1X 8LT

catalyst.coffee | ⊙ catalyst_roasters

9 Caravan Coffee Roasters

The Kiwi-owned collection has brought a slice of NZ coffee and food culture to the capital via its seven restaurants and three brew bars. Visit the redeveloped Victorian warehouse roastery to sample the coffee and pick up brew kit.

Lambworks, North Road, N7 9DP

caravanandco.com | ⊙ caravanroastery

Scenery

171 Union Street, Southwark, SE1 0LN

scenery.coffee

scenerycoffeeroasters

With a combined 30 years of industry experience, Scenery founders Alex, Ross and Stu say the key to success isn't being the cheapest or the most exclusive, but being authentic, transparent and straightforward in their creation of speciality coffee.

It's a noble approach that's made this new roastery in Southwark one to watch. The quality of its coffee has, of course, helped Scenery's upward trajectory and can be roadtested via its core blends as well as a collection of seasonal single origins.

When it comes to sourcing, the trio have a preference for coffees that have undergone experimental processing or which offer higher value for producers at origin. This often translates into rare-find lots that sell out quickly.

'A noble approach that's made this new roastery one to watch'

Scenery HQ is also home to a cafe that deals in banging brews and brunch dishes, which also extends to drinks in the evening and works as an events space.

Established
2023

Roaster make & size
Loring S35 35kg

⑪ Hej Coffee

Mansfield Point, Rodney Road, SE17 1BA

hejcoffee.co.uk | 020 35794663

🔲 hejcoffeeneighbourhood 🔲 hej_coffee

Hej (pronounced 'hey') was conceived in Sweden but born in London, and is a speciality spot comprising two elements: an artisan neighbourhood coffee shop in the front of the building and a sustainable roastery out back.

Get your fika fix at the cafe as you discover a line-up of small-batch coffees divided into three categories: Classics (including house blend Carnival with its dark choc, caramelised almonds and red fruit flavours), Seasonal (including coffees aged in whiskey barrels) and Coffee for Causes (where 30p per kilo sold is donated to charitable organisations). Beans are sourced from sustainable farms in Central and South America and Africa.

Green initiatives run through all aspects of this eco-conscious roastery. Hej uses electric vehicles, carbon-negative coffee bags and a circular bucket system for bulk orders. Working towards B Corp certification, it's also part of the Southwark Climate Collective which aims to make the borough carbon-neutral by 2030.

'Green initiatives run through all aspects of this eco-conscious roastery'

Like what you taste? Get a further fix of Hej at ExCeL London, National Theatre and Unity Place. And keep 'em peeled for the launch of Hej's expanded eco-roastery The London Coffee Factory in Peckham.

Established
2018

Roaster make & size
BESCA BSC-15 15kg

Legs

12 West Lane, Bermondsey, SE16 4NY

coffeelegs.com | 07534 113364

legscoffee

Sprinting onto the London scene in 2024, Anglo-Danish microroastery Legs launched with a mission to provide uber-delicious, bold and interesting coffees.

Innovation is seen as the key to fulfilling this goal. The gang have 20 years' coffee experience yet are tenacious in their desire to remain at the cutting edge of speciality. They roast on an electric fluid-bed machine, in which the beans are suspended in hot air while constantly rotating and mixing. This produces ultra-clean, consistent results – with the bonus that it isn't reliant on gas. The electricity used comes from 100 per cent renewable sources.

'The beans are suspended in hot air while constantly rotating and mixing'

Roasting in small batches means just a handful of the best coffees are in the spotlight at any one time, so the roasters usually showcase a few experimental greens from small plots in their range. This is complemented by a house blend with a Brazilian backbone (the mix changes according to the harvest) and a supporting cast of seasonal single origins from across the globe.

You can taste the beans crafted into quality brews at Legs' coffee shops: NoNo Bermondsey, NoNo Camberwell and the electric NoNo coffee bike outside Bermondsey Station.

Established
2024

Roaster make & size
Typhoon 5kg,
Giesen 15kg

Monmouth Coffee Company

13 Monmouth
Coffee Company

Monmouth started out in Covent Garden in 1978, using direct-flame machines. Nowadays the roastery resides in Bermondsey where the team use energy-efficient Loring air-roasting machines to bronze beans from single farms and co-operatives.

Arch 3, Discovery Estate, St James's Road, SE16 4RA

monmouthcoffee.co.uk | ⊙ monmouthcoffee

14 Dark Arts Coffee

Self-proclaimed coffee alchemist Dark Arts prides itself on 'combining fire, water and magic beans into a divine elixir'. The East London roastery has amassed cult-like status for its ambrosial beans and unholy Insta memes.

1-5 Rosina Street, E9 6JH

darkartscoffee.co.uk | ⊙ darkartscoffee

15 Rascal Coffee

Alexandra Dalton's great-great-great grandfather, Manuel Matheu Ariza, started one of the first coffee farms in Guatemala over 150 years ago. Alexandra continues his legacy by roasting single-origin Guatemalan speciality coffees sourced directly from the farms.

1a Downs Road, Hackney, E5 8QJ

⊙ rascal.coffee | @rascal.coffee

16 Climpson & Sons

From its beginnings as a stall on Broadway Market in 2002, C&S has become a pioneer of the speciality coffee scene. The roastery is bolstered by coffee bars, an academy and The Midnight Oil range of award-winning coffee liqueurs and cocktails.

Leyton, East London

climpsonandsons.com | ⊙ climpsonandsons

Mission Coffee Works

Unit 4, Grosvenor Way, Clapton, E5 9ND

missioncoffeeworks.com | 020 8806 8680

📘 missioncoffeeworks 📷 missioncoffeeworks

Fans of this Clapton roastery are often surprised to learn that the team behind it started out in 2013 serving speciality coffee from a van in Peckham. They fell so head-over-heels with great coffee that, when the opportunity arose in 2015, they took over Mission Coffee Works. From that point, the roastery has been so intrinsically linked with East London's speciality coffee scene that it's hard to picture them ever having done anything other than source and roast the finest greens.

The crew are dedicated to ethical sourcing and quality-led coffee: every aspect of their farm-to-cup business is transparent on pricing, fosters sustainable relationships and supports people and the planet.

'A blend that will impress your coffee snob mates but won't terrify your grandma'

Walking the walk, Mission has planted over 12,000 native trees as part of its collab with Eden Reforestation Projects, and everything that can't be recycled at the roastery is turned into energy. Beans are packed in reusable containers and delivered in an electric van.

Long-lasting relationships with farmers are evidenced in roasts such as Mission's award-winning blend Bells. The Brazilian and Guatemalan coffee reveals notes of chocolate cookie, caramel, almond brittle and is described by the team as a blend that will *'impress your coffee snob mates but won't terrify your grandma.'*

Established
2012

Roaster make & size
Diedrich IR -12 12kg

18 Bad Coffee

Unit 9, Oslo House, Prince Edward Road, Hackney Wick, E9 5LX

drinkbadcoffee.com

badcoffeetastesgood badcoffeetastesgood

It's pretty ballsy calling your business 'Bad' unless you're very good. Luckily, Bad Coffee's co-founder and roaster Mandi Goodier meets the brief (and not just in name). *'We love coffee culture but not in a boring way,'* she says. *'Sure, coffee is about process and brewing, but it's also about meeting a friend for a catch up, fuelling ideas, and being late for work and saying "Fuck it, I may as well grab a flat white".'*

Business partners Mandi and Alex Childs and team work with smallholders in countries including Brazil, Rwanda, Ethiopia, Colombia, Peru and Kenya, aiming to contribute to sustainable agriculture and socio-economic change. All beans sourced are speciality grade, sustainable, traceable and beneficial to all involved. Mandi relies on her instincts when choosing what to roast: *'It's all about finding surprising flavours and making them translatable to everyone. We ain't gatekeepers; we want everyone to enjoy good coffee.'*

Established
2023

Roaster make & size
Roastmax
RMS10 10kg

'Nat Has Her Beans is named after the viral graffiti tag 'Nat Has Herpes''

The roastery only launched in 2023 and is still fizzing with playful enthusiasm. Its decaf, with its zesty chocolate-orange notes is decaffeinated using the sparkling water process, while the Brazilian/Rwandan/Ethiopian house blend, Nat Has Her Beans, is named after the viral graffiti tag 'Nat Has Herpes', which originated in the same building as the roastery.

19 Saint Espresso x Saint Coffee Roasters

13 East Bay Lane, Here East, E20 3BS

saintespresso.com

saintespresso saintespresso

There's no doubting the divine quality of the beans at Hackney's Saint Espresso, as the operation is headed up by reigning two-times UK Coffee Roasting Champion Diana Johnston.

'We're always striving to bring the best to our customers, whether that's in the form of comforting traditional beans, rare finds or even CBD-decaf pods,' says Diana. *'This year we secured a whole nano-lot of naturally processed El Oso. Less than 140kg was produced, contributing to its rarity.'*

'We secured a whole nano-lot of naturally processed El Oso – less than 140kg was produced'

Working with the same producers year after year, to create consistency for customers and build relationships with farmers, is a core part of the Saint approach. The roastery's Angel Espresso (which delivers a full-bodied brew with choc, almond and cherry flavours) is the espresso used across Saint's growing number of coffee bars, and for the last three years has showcased beans from a single producer in southern Brazil: Fernando Beloni. A heavenly host of other beans gives the caffeine curious an opportunity to explore more fruity and floral brews via a rotating signature espresso.

Beyond supporting their farming partners, the team back environmental initiatives such as the El Oso Project, which was set up by importer DRWakefield to support the conservation and protection of natural ecosystems in the Peruvian coffee-growing belt.

Established
2019

Roaster make & size
Giesen W15A 15kg

Publishing that talks to your community

We craft award-winning magazines and contract publishing.

salt

Contact us for a sample pack
saltmedia.co.uk/sample

Hermanos Colombian Coffee Roasters

20 **Hermanos**
Colombian Coffee Roasters

Owners Santiago (pictured), Victor and Adnan started Hermanos to bring their knowledge and the vibrance of Colombian coffee to London. Classic profiles plus seasonal and exotic micro-lots are available across multiple colourful cafes.

Unit 13, Forest Trading Estate, Priestley Way, E17 6AL

hermanoscoffeeroasters.com

hermanoscolombiancoffee

21 **Square Mile**
Coffee Roasters

This multi-award-winning coffee pioneer is synonymous with the capital's coffee culture and has been instrumental in putting London's speciality scene on the world map. Drink its coffees in cafes across the UK and beyond.

Unit 13, Uplands Business Park, Blackhorse Lane, E17 5QJ

shop.squaremilecoffee.com

22 PLOT Roasting

Unit 38, iO Centre, Armstrong Road, Woolwich, SE18 6RS

plotroasting.com | 020 3011 1395

f plotroasting © plotroasting

© Lauren Kallen

A short walk from Woolwich Arsenal Pier is the PLOT Roasting HQ, where a small team create big coffee flavours. *'We named the roastery PLOT because a plot links all the elements of a story,'* says founder Matthew Orchard. *'It's our mission to deliver coffees with character which tell the story of where they were grown and who produced them.'*

The word 'plot' has multiple meanings beyond the narrative of a story, however. It can also refer to plotting data points, such as when the team track temperature changes to form roast profiles. Plots are also the small areas of land where coffee is grown, each affected differently by their specific soil, humidity and altitude.

'A plot links all the elements of a story'

The team source coffee from countries such as Costa Rica, Ecuador, Ethiopia and India to create PLOT's ever-changing line-up of single-origin coffees, as well as its ICON line. The latter is a monthly drop of rare and unique coffees which could include a Colombian geisha brimming with sweet floral notes produced by coffee master Sebastian Ramirez, or a koji-fermented Guatemalan caturra from La Senda.

The team have just launched their new recyclable packaging and are working towards B Corp certification. The roastery also has a focus on education and regularly runs SCA-accredited courses (from beginner to professional level) where coffee fans and aspiring professionals can up their game.

Established
2019

Roaster make & size
Loring S35,
Kestrel 35kg

Elsewhere Coffee

Unit 3, Titan Business Estate, Ffinch Street, SE8 5QA

elsewherecoffee.com

 Elsewhere Coffee Roasters elsewhere_coffee

Dive headfirst into a wonderland of good vibes and cracking brews at Deptford's Elsewhere Coffee, where the team have recently given their roastery HQ a revamp and flung wide its doors to the coffee-loving community.

The high-spec brew bar is now open seven days a week for public training sessions, cuppings, community talks and gigs — as well as to those simply seeking a vibrant spot in South East London at which to slurp quality small-batch coffee.

'Injecting good energy throughout the coffee supply chain'

Opening to the public was the natural next step for the team, whose ethos revolves around cultivating positivity for the people they connect with — both in their locality and in the global communities from which they source beans. Elsewhere trades directly with independent farmers, paying at least 30 per cent above Fairtrade market rates to support growers' wellbeing.

Injecting good energy throughout the supply chain results in banging beans. Heading the diverse line-up is single origin Daydreamer, a smooth sip with notes of milk choc, caramel and cherry acidity that's sourced from family-run Boa Vista farm co-op in Brazil. The price is set by the growers, with profits used to fund community projects, sustainable farming initiatives and education.

Established
2018

Roaster make & size
Probat P12 12kg

NOTES

Somewhere to keep a record of exceptional beans and brews you've discovered on your coffee adventures

NOTES

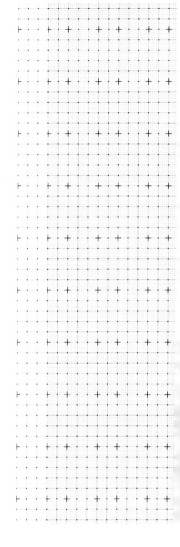

INDEX

FOR
BREW
FRE
&BEA
GEEK